WHICH DOG
— FOR ME? —

"How about a box of Cockers?"

KW-227

A gaggle of "gray ghosts"—Weimaraner puppies. This old-time German breed of working gun dog also makes an affectionate family pet.

Title page: With a spotted past and a surging future, the Dalmatian breed offers pet owners a reliable and handsome companion dog.

Photography credits: Tom Caravaglia , Mary Jane Carberry, Rhonda Dalton, Isabelle Français, Joseph Hartnagle, Laakso, Celeste Meade, Diane Pearce, Robert Pearcy, Ron Reagan, Vince Serbin, Sally Anne Thompson.

Distributed in the UNITED STATES by T.F.H. Publications, Inc., One T.F.H. Plaza, Neptune City, NJ 07753; in CANADA to the Pet Trade by H & L Pet Supplies Inc., 27 Kingston Crescent, Kitchener, Ontario N2B 2T6; Rolf C. Hagen Ltd., 3225 Sartelon Street, Montreal 382 Quebec; in CANADA to the Book Trade by Macmillan of Canada (A Division of Canada Publishing Corporation), 164 Commander Boulevard, Agincourt, Ontario M1S 3C7; in ENGLAND by T.F.H. Publications, PO Box 15, Waterlooville PO7 6BQ; in AUSTRALIA AND THE SOUTH PACIFIC by T.F.H. (Australia) Pty. Ltd., Box 149, Brookvale 2100 N.S.W., Australia; in NEW ZEALAND by Ross Haines & Son, Ltd., 82 D Elizabeth Knox Place, Panmure, Auckland, New Zealand; in the PHILIPPINES by Bio-Research, 5 Lippay Street, San Lorenzo Village, Makati, Rizal; in SOUTH AFRICA by Multipet Pty. Ltd., P.O. Box 35347, Northway, 4065, South Africa. Published by T.F.H. Publications, Inc. Manufactured in the United States of America by T.F.H. Publications, Inc.

WHICH DOG
— FOR ME? —

by James Johnson and Andrew DePrisco

WHICH DOG FOR ME?

INTRODUCTION

Why buy a dog? A quality companion, a capable guardsman, a playmate and part-time babysitter for the toddler, a hunter or duck toter, a reliable jogging mate, a lap-trained doll, or a cat disciplinarian? All certainly reasonable reasons. *Everyone* owns a dog, so why shouldn't I? Puppies are cute, irresistible to women, and great conversation pieces, provided they never grow up.

Owning a *purebred* dog is chic, a pristine yuppie expression of comfort and decisiveness—pedigree-

Never be swayed by the cuteness of a puppy, especially one as tantalizing as a baby Shar-Pei.

dropping at pool parties: "My purebred Chinese Shar-Pei, Wun-Lee Wing-Ding of MooGooGaiPan, is a great nephew, once-removed, of Sugar Daddy . . . you know the dog on that episode of *Hill Street Blues*." However, when Wing-Ding whizzes on the newly imported Oriental carpet, makes chop suey of your new Danielle Steele novella and is no longer wrinkly and adorable, pedigree-dropping may fall on deaf ears.

"Why ever did I get this baneful imp bent on destruction? What an awful breed! Who would intentionally breed such horrors?"

What are your reasons for wanting or needing a dog? Your reasons and living conditions are key to choosing the right breed for you. Living in the close confines of the Bronx or Tokyo, you'll need a compact, easy-clean, biddable dog. While the Maltese is grand in its compactness and obedience, traipsing his luxurious white coat across an unswept E168th Street will be the matty, muddy death of his floor-length fur. There are more ideal choices: a Smooth Fox Terrier or a Schipperke or maybe a Japanese Shiba Inu.

There are breeds to fulfill anyone's requirement, and they vary tremendously from a six-pound fur-ridden hell-bound dervish to a 200-pound mush-faced, soft-hearted throb of a man-stopper. Of course, appearance is not enough and the dog's individual requirements, contingent

Size, temperament and ability vary from breed to breed: both the Boxer and the Shiba Inu can make fabulous choices for the right family.

on his size, temperament and in-bred tendencies, play a major role in your deciding on a breed of dog. Although the easygoing houndy appearance of the Black and Tan Coonhound may drop your socks, if you don't have the space or time to exercise such a rambunctiously energetic dog, you're baying up the wrong tree.

Owning a dog—any dog—is a real responsibility. While a cat, bird, or hamster may survive a couple days without attention, a dog *cannot* be left alone for more than a few hours. Dogs are children: they must be fed, potty-trained, cleaned, taught, schooled and given guidance and attention. Raising a puppy

into a dog you can live with is a feat that requires a little know-how, patience and a lot of love.

However, dog-ownership responsibilities begin before you phone the first breeder or browse through a pet shop. The kind of dog you want should not be a serendipitous or even unlucky event. More than any other species on earth, domestic canines vary in size, shape, color and disposition. There're many kinds and breeds of dog to choose from—which do you *like*, find appealing, endearing, intriguing? Remember too that your living conditions and lifestyle may limit the possibilities. As stunning and noble as you find the Irish Wolfhound, he'll curl up his

Introduction

36-inches of noble tallness and die in your two-room studio. Likewise, the Pug and Pomeranian make great watchdogs, but they'll never protect your family of eight from the window-framed prowler.

Since the beginning of time, man and the dog have been inseparable. Dogs actually enjoy serving man—and man, never looking a gift-mutt in the muzzle—has found a myriad of ways for dogs to help. Through the millenia, dogs have provided means of transport over sand, snow and space; protected sheep, children and kings; carried messages, diseases and good fortune; sought out mines, lost travellers, drugs and thieves; moved herds, carts and judges' heads; retrieved downed geese and other birds, slippers and drunken seamen; run down hares, slaves, and handlers; warmed hands, bellies, hearts and homes.

Man has intentionally bred for the characteristics and traits he desired in the dog. It is no miracle nor mystery that the right dog is out there, since we've engineered the canine, with or without his blessing, to assume most any form. Breeds, usually, don't just happen. When ranchers decided that a mid-size, hard-biting dog was vital to maneuvering the chattle cattle to market, they set about creating it; when castle-kept eunuchs learned that the Empress desired her dogs to look like Lilliputian lions, they too got to work; and when British or Chinese agents

Canines as large as miniature horses require a lot from an owner. Imagine the accommodations required to keep four such equine wonders!

decided that a dog with uneven jaws and a wide skull could better hold a bull's snout and an audience's attention, they bred for it. So today we have cattle drovers, leonine lap dogs, and undershot bulldogs, and we use them and show them and share our homes with them.

The authors contend, too, that owners can find a suitable companion dog from the non-pedigree dogs available at local humane societies. Considering the number of homeless, lost, abandoned and mistreated dogs there are in society, adopting a mutt is a noble option for some. Quality purebred dogs, particularly those from proven pedigree lines and of the rarer breeds, will not be inexpensive to acquire. Pet shops

Chow Chow puppies to plush up anyone's Christmas stocking. Remember that live animals under a yuletide tree cannot be returned if they don't fit!

may be helpful in directing interested parties to reliable sources of mutts, mongrels and moggies. Do not totally discount the worth of a mixed–breed dog, since most any dog, properly trained and cared for, can make an exceptional pet. For those who are inclined strictly towards purebreds, from the wonderful breeds that come down to us through history, choose carefully, sensibly and realistically, but most of all be responsible in deciding *Which Dog For Me?*

The Affenpinscher is a most adaptable small dog who enjoys monkeying around with the right gentle owner.

AFFENPINSCHER

This peculiar tiny terrier dog whose origins trace to seventeenth-century Germany stands less than ten inches high. For its miniature size, the Affenpinscher possesses a large head whose facial expression has been referred to as "monkey-like" through the ages. While solid black colored dogs are favored by show people, black and tan, red and gray colored dogs are available too. The coat is hard and wiry and longer on the legs and head.

Although the breed has been recognized in the United States since the mid-1930s, the Affen has never been terribly popular. Unlike many other toy dogs, this feisty moustached companion is plucky and a true terrier, though he appreciates gentle care and affection. Rough treatment can provoke stubbornness and long periods alone can break the breed's centerstage spirit. Ideal for an apartment dweller or a person on-the-go who wishes to tote his tot along.

AFGHAN HOUND

An ancient breed of running hound, the Afghan stands a tall 25–27 inches. His lithe construction can be rather deceiving, for he is a well-muscled, solidly constructed dog who weighs 50–60 pounds. Adorned with a long, silky straight coat, which is short on the face, the Afghan occurs in a great variety of colors and combinations; the one color objection is white on the head. In general appearance, the Afghan is considered aristocratic, dignified, and proud.

As a sighthound whose ancestors scaled the unfenced deserts, the Afghan obviously needs space to run. Although this chic, luxuriously coated, strong dog turns heads in the city, he is more appropriately suited to suburban or country life. Grooming is a chore and must be introduced very early on for a full-grown Afghan, a mass of tangles and matts, unwilling to sit, would be most difficult. Not as quick to learn as they are to run and potentially stubborn and aloof, Afghan Hounds need owners ready to commit to their training and care. These dominant dogs may not accept other pets in their homes.

AIREDALE TERRIER

Tracing his origin to an extinct working terrier type commonly referred to as the English Black and Tan Terrier, the Airedale can be a height of 23 inches for males, and a weight of around 44 pounds. His color is, not unlike his forefathers', black and tan saddled. The head is well balanced, suggestive of intelligence, strength, and great determination. Stance and movement, too, should be smooth, steady and strong. The Airedale sports a dense, wiry, and hard outer jacket.

Although the largest of the terrier breeds, the Airedale only ranks with medium-sized dogs. Nevertheless these are active, athletic dogs that need ample outside time, preferably a fenced-in yard or running pen. Today the Airedale is prized for his handsome looks, though as a working terrier years ago, this was not true. Present-day owners subscribe to visits to the grooming parlor since clipping keeps the dog looking his best. Airedales are smart and trainable enough for most any chore, and are recommended for the owner looking for a kind, noble and versatile purebred.

An ancient wind hound, the Afghan Hound is a hardy outdoorsman and the showiest of show dogs.

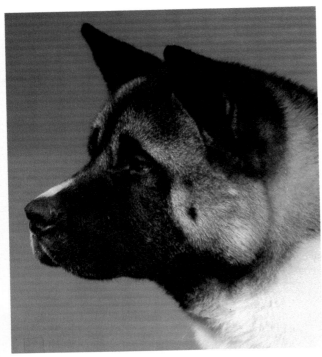

The Akita ranks among the largest and most stylish of purebred dogs: he is rightly named a national treasure of Japan.

AKITA

This Japanese national treasure possesses a centuries-old rich and regal ancestry as a hunter and companion. The Akita today is a large, substantially boned, and very strong (and strong-willed) dog. Dogs never under 25 inches; bitches never less than 23. Weight typically between 75–110 pounds. The breed's erect ears, somewhat small in relation to the overall head; large, full tail, carried over the back; and thick, dense double coat are all "Northern-breed" characteristics that endear the Akita to many. Coat color can be any, including white and pinto.

As a sizable dog, the Akita has a similarly sized attitude, a true big-dog approach to life. Thus owners are advised to be assertive in handling the dog-in-training. The breed's typical Japanese temperament—stubborn and ever so smart—coupled with the dog's size makes this a lot of dog for any owner. Exercise and consistent attention are musts for the Akita. Aggressive, unkind treatment, inappropriate for any dog, will especially ruin this dignified and centered animal.

ALASKAN MALAMUTE

The ancient ancestors of the Alaskan Malamute were Arctic sled dogs of the native Innuit tribe called Mahlemuts. True to the type in work ethic and endurance, the Malamute is composed of heavy (not coarse) bone and solid muscle. The head is broad and powerful, though not cobby or coarse. The ears are upstanding triangles, small in proportion to the overall head. Chest, strong and deep. Color can be black or shades of gray, with lighter mask and underbody common. Males typically 25 inches, 85 pounds; bitches 23 inches, 75 pounds.

A generally easy-care family dog, the Alaskan Malamute is a devoted companion animal with an extroverted, hardworking approach to the world around him. These dogs enjoy working, playing, and eating, as well as being around their loving families. Grooming needs are moderate but constant. Owners living in hot climates should not consider the Malamute, a dog that is more at home in igloos than beach houses.

AMERICAN ESKIMO

Sporting a long, thick, straight coat, the American Eskimo traces undoubtedly to Northern dogs, evidenced also in the small upstanding triangular ears and carried-over-the-back tail. Preferred coat color is white, though white with biscuit or cream can also be found. The American Eskimo is broken down by height: Standard, 14–19 inches;

A champion snow and ice dog, the Alaskan Malamute is an affectionate workhorse of a husky.

Miniature, 11–15 inches; Toy, males less than 12, females less than 11 inches. The Standard and Miniatures are the older dogs, having been bred since at least the early twentieth century.

A well-adjusted American Eskimo is a calm, biddable and beautiful pet. Owners must be willing to be consistent and patient when opting to take on a dog of spitz origins. Spitz dogs in general require encouragement and time in order for an owner to convince them of their place. Praise is essential. These happy, bold and super-smart dogs

A traditional American purebred, the American Eskimo, once called simply Spitz, is an elegant and intelligent dog.

AMERICAN PIT BULL TERRIER

This potent blend of old bulldog (used for bull baiting) and terrier (used for ratting) was fused to battle other dogs of the same hard-as-nails alloy. Necessarily, great determination, strength and stamina were requisite breeding priorities. The "trait" or characteristic of "gameness" served (and often still serves) as the single-most important quality in the breed. Size varies considerably, with 18–22 inches, 50–80 pounds being more a median than a mean. Ears are often cropped, though need not be. Tails are typically not docked. All colors are possible.

Buyer beware! This recognized breed of the United Kennel Club has stirred great controversy in the world dog community. Although this is the same dog that Spanky and Alfalfa knocked about with, those black-and-white gay days are long past and today's breed has been corrupted by some and mauled by others. A well-bred Pit Bull Terrier is the kindest, most loyal of dogs, though always aggressive towards other dogs, as is true to its history. Certain American locales as well as England have banned "pit bulls" due to the high risk of aggression and viciousness. Proper training, although completely essential, is

enjoy being outside, though they are amenable to living in apartments provided ample exercise time is allotted. The breed is strictly American since England recognizes the German Spitzen, which are most similar to the Eskies. Toys (batteries not included) may not be available as readily as the larger two varieties.

secondary to proper breeding and rearing, and smaller dogs are preferable for the potential owner.

AMERICAN STAFFORDSHIRE TERRIER

This bull-and-terrier creation, tracing to the Staffordshire Terriers of England, was first brought to the U.S. in the mid-1800s as a fighting dog. American breeders selected for increased size, and today the AmStaff stands 17–19 inches tall and weighs 40–50 pounds. The head, impressive in size, is marked by a broad skull and defined muscle. Neck, muscular, as is body throughout. Chest, deep and broad. Coat is short, close, and stiff to the touch. All solid, parti, and patched colors occur. Ears are often cropped, though need not be. Tail, short and straight, is not docked.

A noble, well-respected member of the dog-show community, the AmStaff can too easily be mistaken for the U.K.C.-registered Pit Bull Terrier, so owners must be cognizant that this is practically the same dog, though hopefully more reliably bred than many so-called Pit Bull Terriers. These are very powerful and able-minded dogs that need exercise and attention. Cats and other dogs are not recommended for owners.

Properly trained and responsibly cared for, the American Staffordshire Terrier makes a quality companion for children.

AMERICAN WATER SPANIEL

This all-American hunting dog was developed in the late nineteenth century to work on waterfowl. The American Water Spaniel sports a thick, very protective jacket of closely knit curls, said to have a marcel effect. Facial hair is short. Of medium size, the breed stands 15–18 inches in height and weighs 25–45 pounds. The overall head is moderate in size. The body, sturdy and strong, should not be too compact and never coarse. Colors are solid liver and dark chocolate, possibly with a touch of white on the chest.

Good-tempered and athletic, the American Water Spaniel is a working hunting dog that is most uncommonly kept by pet owners and show-dog people. These are handsome dogs and most unexaggerated in appearance. Breeders rarely sell

Australian Cattle Dog

dogs to non-hunters, and owners seeking a spaniel for pet purposes should consider any of the less-work-oriented sporting dogs first, namely the cockers and springers.

AUSTRALIAN CATTLE DOG

Herdsmen of Australia required a truly enduring dog to work their unruly cattle and sheep over the punishing terrain of the land Down Under. No-nonsense, the AuCaDo stands 17–20 inches and packs 35–45 pounds of raw muscle and bone. Coat is medium-short, harsh, straight and dense; colors include blue-speckled, with black, blue or tan markings on the head; and red-speckled, with darker red markings on the head. White specimens oc-

cur but are not accepted by registries.

This Aussie amalgam of the very best ingredients is truly a remarkable purebred for the owner looking for an all-around working dog as well as a commonsense companion. As a herding dog for cows or sheep, the Australian Cattle Dog bows to no dog—he is tireless and industrious. Of course, owners must require an active, protective, and vehement canine to consider the AuCaDo.

AUSTRALIAN KELPIE

Created from a smooth-haired Scotch collie type, the Australian Kelpie is 100-percent working dog. Height: 17–20 inches. Weight:

Australian Cattle Dogs work hard for their daily bread: these primitive herding dogs take their designated duties with religious austerity.

25–45 pounds. He is built for agility, stamina, and *work*. His construction is lithe and hard, with a slightly rounded head, prick ears, and an overall rather foxlike countenance. Chest is deep rather than wide; tail hangs slightly curved at rest, moderately higher in excitement. The coat is double, short, and dense, occurring in black, red (either with or without tan), fawn, chocolate, and smoke blue.

A true favorite in his native Australia, the Kelpie has been accurately described as a workaholic with a herding propensity second to none, effective on any livestock. No sturdier, more adaptable "domestic" dog exists, and the Kelpie could survive in rainforest or ice tundra, though he'd prefer a climate somewhere in the middle for sure. Owners seeking solely a pet dog should not consider this avid herding dog, despite his truly utilitarian abilites.

AUSTRALIAN SHEPHERD

The Aussie's origin traces to France, and, despite its name, Australia was but a brief stop in this dog's history. Developed in America from crosses of the original French dogs and various collie types working in America, the Aussie today remains a hardy, untiring working dog, excellent with the herd. A mid-sized dog at 18–23 inches and 35–70 pounds, the Australian Shepherd sports an array of colors, including blue merle, red (liver) merle, black, liver, red, with or without white and/

The ranch worker of the American West, the Australian Shepherd is the number one herding dog of the United States, and he's pretty too!

or tan markings. Eye color may be brown, blue, flecked or odd-eyed (one blue and one brown).

No dog as well-rounded, intelligent and pretty as the Australian Shepherd could stay out of the public eye for long. Of course, the Australian Shepherd is no new breed and has been used extensively by American ranch workers for many years. Owners must be able to give this driven herding dog a job! As a pet, the Aussie is as affectionate as he is energetic, so lots of love and labor once again go hand in hand.

A unique and sensitive purebred, the Basenji derives from ancient African lines and is most noted for its aloof air and peculiar yodel-like voice.

AUSTRALIAN TERRIER

Developed Down Under as a watchdog and vermin deterrent, this high-spirited dog stands a mere 10 inches, and weighs between 12–14 pounds. Head is long and flat-skulled; body is low-set and slightly longer than high. Coat length is about 2.5 inches, and texture is harsh, straight, and dense. Color may be blue-black or silver-black, with rich tan markings on head and legs; sandy; or clear red.

Not to be confused with the Silky Terrier (also of Australia), the Australian Terrier is no toy but rather a hardbitten hedge hunter with a propensity towards ratting. Although the breed's instincts are rather intact, it makes a fine companion dog that is affectionate to children and adults alike. As smallish terriers go, without entering the world of munchkin munchers (the toys), the Australian Terrier is a solid choice.

BASENJI

One of the few purebred dogs to emerge from Africa, the Basenji, or "barkless dog," first entered the West in the late 1800s. Standing about 16–17 inches and weighing merely 22–24 pounds, the Basenji is distinctive in appearance—the breed has a wrinkled forehead; flat, tapering skull; and small, pointed, erect ears. Swift, graceful motion is characteristic. The body is short. Tail is carried tightly over to either side of the body. Coat short, silky, with very pliant skin. Colors include red, black,

black and tan, and brindle, all with white feet, chest, and tail tip.

A sharp and clean purebred dog, the Basenji resides as one of the most unique of all domesic canines. For reasons not entirely known, the Basenji is "barkless" and therefore does not make a great alarm dog, additionally it is too small to be a guard dog. Therefore, this yodelling medium-sized African cannot feign to be anything other than a terrific pet and show dog. Cat lovers have found themselves enamored of the Basenji, as they are great self-groomers and uncannily intelligent. Training requires patience and nothing impresses a Basenji more than constant praise.

BASSET HOUND

With his soulful eyes and short "crooked" legs, the centuries-old Basset Hound moves with deliberate, though never clumsy, motion. Standing 14 inches or less and weighing a substantial 40–60 pounds, the Basset Hound is the "heaviest-boned" dog in dogdom. Large, well-proportioned head, marked by soft, sad eyes; extremely long, low-set ears, and pronounced dewlap are his highly recognizable features. Any hound color, typically lemon and white (bicolor) or black, white and tan (tricolor), is common on this short and smooth-coated canine.

The Basset Hound should be well

The Basset Hound has long been a favorite choice for pet owners. Today's Basset may not take to the hot or cold trail, but has retained its fabulous howl and cavernous bark.

Beagle

conditioned and given plenty of opportunity to exercise. Owners must take the responsibility to encourage these dogs to move, as laziness and stubbornness come with Basset territory. Instinctually the Basset still has a nose for the hunt and proves eager and willing. A popular companion and show dog, the Basset often excels in field trials and instinct tests as well.

BEAGLE

Although the British claim the Beagle as their own, and approach Beagling with splendid sportsman-like pagentry, America—the land of

With the right encouragement and a steady hand, the Beagle can take well to the show ring.

Snoopy—also avidly reveres this little foxhound. Conveniently sized in two varieties: under 13 inches; and 13–15 inches (16 in Britain). The versatile and hardy Beagle is solidly constructed; with a short, strong back; muscular shoulders; and deep, broad chest. Head construction allows plenty of "brain room"; ears, moderately long, broad; eyes, large (said to be gentle and pleading). Coat is invariably short, smooth and dense. Incidentally, Pocket Beagles (about six inches in height) occur and are propagated by some fanciers.

These are generally clean, even-tempered, affectionate dogs that thrive on the company of people and other dogs. Housebreaking efforts must be concentrated; praise abundant and reprimand soft but consistent; training in general must be firm but kind. Discipline can break the merry spirit of the Beagle, so moderation is key. Dogs should be given good time for exercise, and contact with other dogs helps to elicit the true gregarious hound spirit of the breed: a stray canary may also make a good buddy for a Beagle.

BEARDED COLLIE

Inarguably an ancient breed, the Bearded Collie was developed (or evolved) centuries ago on the British Isles as a superb herding dog, and later a drover. A survivor of the rough Highlands of Scotland, the Beardie sports a long and lean, though very strong and muscular, construction. Adorned abundantly with beard and moustache, the head of the Beardie gives an expression that is said to distinguish this breed from all others. Coat is double, with the outercoat flat, hard, strong and shaggy; and the undercoat soft. Color can be black, blue, brown, or

learns the rules of the house quickly, too much confinement can deflate its jovial temperament. Grooming on a weekly basis avoids knots and kinks in the coat. Popular in the British Isles for centuries, the Beardie continues to gain admirers in North America for all the right reasons.

The Bearded Collie has much to recommend it to modern-day dog folk on both sides of the Atlantic.

fawn, with or without white markings (coat color may lighten with maturity).

Bouncy well describes this good-hearted sheepdog who is especially fond of children. The Bearded Collie makes a great family dog and is recommended for other-than-apartment living. Although the breed

BEDLINGTON TERRIER

Undaunted and enduring, this ton of terrier must not be weighed by his soft lamblike appearance. Measuring 15–17.5 inches and weighing a lean 17–23 pounds, the Bedlington Terrier conceals mustard and spice under its mixture of hard and soft hair, standing well out from the skin. This distinct coat is referred to as "crisp" to the touch and has a tendency to curl. The head is narrow, but deep and rounded; ears triangular with rounded tips. Tail, described

21

as scimitar-shaped, tapers to a point. Though the unknowing may perceive a Bedlington as white, the actual coat colors are labeled blues, tans and sandies.

A sophisticated, affectionate gentleman's terrier, the Bedlington,

BELGIAN SHEEPDOGS: GROENENDAEL, LAEKENOIS, MALINOIS, AND TERVUREN

Long extant on the fields of Belgium, four distinct varieties of shepherd dog share renowned reputations as serious and acutely intelli-

in blue or gray, is guaranteed to brighten any owner's blue or gray day. This smallish terrier is as energetic and alert as he is unique and courageous. Somewhat elitist perhaps, Bedlingtons generally prefer the mature sensible company of adults. Grooming demands have simplified through the years, though the dog still requires professional clipping or scissoring to project the classic Bedlington air.

The most popular of the four Belgian Sheepdogs, the solid black Groenendael is biddable and not too difficult to acquire.

gent working dogs. Differing only in coat type and color, the Belgian Sheepdogs stand ideally 22–26 inches at the shoulders and weigh in the 60–65- pound category. The Belgian Sheepdog, Groenendael, sports a medium-long coat that is invariably colored in black. The Laekenois, coated shaggily in rough, harsh 2.25-inch hair, occurs in various shades of fawn to mahogany, with black overlay, and bears a very distinct appearance. The Malinois also occurs in fawn to mahogany, with black overlay, but his coat is moderately short and dense and not harsh or rough. The Tervuren wears a medium-long coat, colored in fawn through mahogany, with black overlay.

For dog people looking for a police dog look-alike, the Belgian Sheepdogs or Shepherds have frequently been compared to the more popular German Shepherd Dog. The four Belgian breeds offer owners certain unforeseen advantages, as these dogs are sizable, intelligent, free-thinking, easycare and extremely trainable. The more popular of the four, the Groenendael and Tervuren, have made quite the splash with American owners, and all four breeds are super-effective guard dogs. The long-coated Terv and wire Laeken require some coat attention, though all four require little in terms of maintenance, other than exercise, of course.

BERNESE MOUNTAIN DOG

Distinguished by his long silky coat, the Bernese Mountain Dog is one of four extant varieties of Swiss mountain dogs, who trace their lineage back to Roman dogs of war, brought through the region by the invading legions. This large, sturdy and intelligent working dog possesses strong bone, much muscle, and great agility. The skull is broad and flat, with ears triangular in shape, and eyes dark brown in color. Tail is bushy, carried low when the dog is relaxed, and possibly swirling upward when alert. The coat is thick, moderately long, and may be either straight or slightly wavy. Color is classic Swiss: a jet black ground color with rich rust and clear white markings. Nose, always black.

Gaining much ground in the purebred world is the Bernese Mountain Dog. This medium-sized dog excels in affection and obedience, not to mention good looks.

This outgoing working dog is both sweet-natured and good-looking. The Berner continues to gain headway in the United States and has been widely promoted as a terrific family dog. Owners must be cautioned about not overfeeding the puppy and to maintaining a good exercise routine. The long coat requires a quick brushing but is thankfully dirt-resistant.

BICHON FRISE

At first sight a toy, this gundog-gone-small sports (or "non-sports") a sturdy construction and the hardy temperament of his game-chasing ancestors. The texture of the abundant Bichon coat is strongly considered by fanciers; the undercoat should be soft and dense, with the outer coat coarser and curlier, together creating a plush or velvet feel. Bichons may be white, with or without shadings of buff, cream or apricot around the ears or on the body. Standing only 9–12 inches at the shoulders, the Bichon carries his plumed tail gaily over his back, and his dark eyes and nose complete the general impression of the jaunty and jubilant Bichon Frise.

Not much of a "powder puff," the Bichon Frise is an active, lively dog sometimes improperly assigned to the dog-world "toy box." Too large to be rightly dubbed a toy dog, the Bichon is an adaptable breed able to thrive in most any environment, given ample attention and exercise. If grooming a dog is not your bag, don't buy a Bichon. The coat is so very important to the dog's appearance, standing off from the body with a soft undercoat. Daily grooming, therefore, must be encouraged.

BLACK AND TAN COONHOUND

Constructed to endure the elements and all other demands of the trail, the Black and Tan stands 23–27 inches of power, agility, and alertness. The distinctive head should be clean (well-sculpted and free from folds); ears, low set and reaching well beyond the tip of the nose when extended; and the flews should be developed in typical hound fashion. Coat is short and dense, offering sufficient protection. Color is invariably a deep black with rich tan markings.

Once considered solely a hunter's dog, the Black and Tan has a growing following in the show ring and pet world. The breed's hunting instincts are still very strong, and owners are urged to give the dogs appropriate outlets for their drive. Like most other coonhounds, the Black and Tan enjoys the company of kids as well as other pets, though small raccoon-like domesticated mammals may pose a problem for even the mildest of Black and Tans.

BLOODHOUND

Tracing far back into man's history, the Bloodhound breed has doggedly traced and tracked with his most discriminating nose. Standing a hardy 23–27 inches, and weigh-

Renowned for its white full coat and gentle expression, the Bichon Frise abounds in clouds of personality too.

ing a substantial 70–110 pounds, the Bloodhound sports a short, thick and hard coat, colored in black and tan, red and tan, or tawny, with a small amount of white on the chest, feet, and tip of tail allowed. A most markedly houndy hound, the breed is very powerful, stands over much ground, and possesses abundant loose skin, especially on the head and neck. Ears are thin, soft, and extremely long. Tail is long and tapering, set rather high.

This ancient country bumpkin is as well mannered and polite as a dog can be. The dogs have unusually keen scenting instincts and are much too large to confine indoors for any length of time. Tracking events sponsored by breed clubs or a similar search and rescue escapade will bring great pleasure to both dog and owner. The dog's need

ing 30–45 pounds. Coat occurs in two varieties: medium-long attaining lengths to three inches; and smooth. In both types, the topcoat is thick and straight, with undercoat soft and dense. Various colors with white occur, though black, blue,

for exercise is tremendous though appetites are not nearly as voracious as other dogs this size. While grooming needs are minimal, cleaning the ears and flews (especially on hungry puppies) is necessary.

A classic purebred that traces to saints and sinners, the Bloodhound boasts the species's best nose and a patient temperament befitting a saint.

BORDER COLLIE

A true herder if ever there was one, the perfectly balanced Border Collie lives solely for the task at hand. He is a medium-sized dog, standing 18–20 inches and weigh-

chocolate, red are most common; additionally, merle can occur in all colors. A doggy dog, the skull is fairly broad, muzzle tapering, ears medium sized and carried erect or semi-erect, tail moderately long and well coated.

Considered by its advocates as the "real collie" and the hardest working and most talented of all herding dogs, the Border Collie enjoys a wide following in England and a healthy one in the United States. These are the dogs of sheepmen and excel in obedience and sheepdog trials like no other. Their energy and instincts are irrepressible; nonetheless, the Border is a close-bonding pet, and given proper outlets with organized trials and the like, the Border can make a smashing companion animal.

Great Britain's prized sheepdog does well in America too; though not frequent at dog shows, the Border Collie is a popular choice of ranchers.

BORDER TERRIER

If an ounce of pluck is worth a pound of luck, the tireless Border Terrier is one lucky dog. Standing only 10 inches at the shoulder and weighing about a dozen pounds, this rough- and wiry-coated dog exercises great agility and courage with his medium-boned, strongly put-together body. His characteristic "otter head," narrow shoulders and body, moderately short thick tail make him stand out clearly from his terrier cousins. Color can be red, grizzle and tan, blue and tan, or wheaten.

A terrier of convenience for those looking for a small working dog with easycare features. Unlike many other terriers, the Border does not require stripping. His showing potential, due to his alert manner and

his overall obedient tendencies, endears the Border to most persons who favor terriers as companion animals.

neck and jaws, and very deep, though narrow chest. The skull is long and narrow; ears are small and lie back on the neck when relaxed;

BORZOI

This noble Russian running hound, known also as the Russian Wolfhound, has been coursing wolves in his homeland since the 1600s. Standing a tall 28–31 inches, the Borzoi denotes strength, courage, and agility in his lithe construction. Particularly outstanding qualities include long powerful legs, strong

The elegant and eminently graceful Borzoi excels in the show ring and makes an even-tempered companion, requiring much respect and time.

eyes, dark in color, offer an intelligent, rather soft appearance. Coat is long and silky, either flat, wavy, or rather curly; it is short and smooth on the head, ears, and front of the legs. Any color or combination of colors occur, often with white predominating.

Over the centuries there have been a whole pack of reasons to own a Borzoi, as many a Russian with bothersome wolves in his life will contest. Today, however, the reasons are fewer and maybe more frivolous (though Russian wolf-coursing pageants leave us with doubt). Elegance comes in no finer nor larger package. The Borzoi requires a lot of space to move his very long legs, plus much grooming and a he-man's portion of borscht at supper.

BOSTON TERRIER

Born on the East coast of the U.S.A., the Boston Terrier resulted from a blending of various bulldog and bull-and-terrier types. He has a short smooth jacket that well reveals his solid frame and substantial musculature. Skull is square in outline, flat on top and free from wrinkles; muzzle is short, square, wide and deep; eyes, set wide apart; ears, carried erect, either cropped or left natural. The short tail can be either straight or "screw," more like a corkscrew perhaps. Height: 15–17 inches. Preferred color is brindle with white markings, but black with the same markings are seen.

An American tradition, like apple pie and tax evasion, not dating back as far as that city's tea party, the

America's gentleman terrier, the Boston Terrier is a smart-sized, affectionate purebred choice.

Boston delights his lifelong owners with his gentlemanly ways, few demands and handsome looks. Plus the Boston is ideally sized and takes care of himself. He is a popular choice of mature fanciers and quite long-lived.

BOUVIER DES FLANDRES

This Belgian breed stems from a long ancestry of hard-working, hard-bitten cattle herders and cart pullers. A rather sizable and sturdy dog standing 22.5–27.5 inches, the Bouvier presents a rugged and downright impressive appearance. Head is large, and well adorned with prominent eyebrows, beard and moustache; ears are placed high and alert. Coat is medium in length (about 2.5 inches), double, and tousled. Color can be any from fawn through black, including pepper and salt, gray, and brindle.

Still popular in Belgium, Holland, and France today, the Bouvier has adapted well to contemporary life and is a top-notch guard dog who can be trained for man-stopper/ schutzhund work. This medium-sized dog with big-dog potential as a guard offers reason enough for many to welcome this bearded bloke into their homes.

BOXER

Refined and most sophisticated, the Boxer stems from a well-concocted mixture of nearly every rough and scrappy bulldog of Europe long ago. Standing 22.5–25 inches at the shoulders, this squarely built dog possesses sturdy bone, strong limbs, and a short tightly fitting coat. The breed's head is closely considered by breed connoisseurs: it must be harmoniously proportioned, clean, and strong. Ears may be cropped or left in their natural state. Bite is normally undershot. Chest is deep and of fair width; the body is considerably refined overall. Tail is docked short, as much a necessity as a style. Possible colors are fawn or brindle.

A prominent, smart choice of dog lovers, the Boxer assuredly is a knockout of a pet and home guardian. An animal as powerful and sizable as the Boxer fortunately is sweet-tempered and closely bonding with his entire family. The breed's talents have lured him into such circles as police and military work as well as therapy and assistance dogs. Boxers are superlative with kids, accepting of cats and other animals, and don't drool on either.

BRIARD

A very old working dog native to France, the Briard impresses one immediately with its distinctive appearance. The Briard is coated in long (generally six inches or more on the shoulders), slightly wavy, quite stiff fur. Head is long and quite wide, but should never appear cumbersome. Ears, thick in leather, should be set high; when alert, carried upright. Tail, well feathered, is not docked; and it forms a crook at its end. The Briard stands 23–27 inches tall and totes a hearty 75 pounds of substance. With the exception of white, all uniform colors are acceptable.

Despite his flowing locks, the Briard is a most confident and courageous canine who has proven himself in may arenas. He abounds in possibilities for an owner searching for a personable, identifiable dog. Their devotion to their masters and ability to defend their home are

The Boxer, less a fighter than a lover, enjoys the reputation of being one of the most family-oriented and soft-hearted of the effective guardian breeds.

conceivably boundless. Certain breeders stress the strong need for human socialization at a young age.

BRITTANY

Too small to be a setter and too leggy to be a spaniel, the Brittany is quite simply the Brittany—a versatile, resourceful hunter and a loyal, intelligent companion. A French native, this tailless gundog (the tail is naturally not more than four inches long) stands 19–20 inches tall and weighs between 35–40 pounds. His medium-length coat lies flat and is fine in texture; may tend toward the wavy, with a small amount of fringe on the ears, underside, and back of the legs. In the U.S., accepted colors are orange and white and liver and white, though international and French standards also allow black and white and tricolor; while ticking may be present, clear colors are preferred by show people.

Few hunting dogs challenge the abilities of the Brittany. Likewise, he is renowned for his keen pet possibilities and is a favorite as both hunter and companion the world over. This is an easily trained, conveniently sized, flashy dog with a real flare for family life.

BRUSSELS GRIFFON

Whether sporting a long, hard, wiry coat or a short dense jacket (a variety also known as the Petit Brabaçon), the Brussels Griffon was once a fashionable riding companion about town with most any cabby in Belgium. His head is large and round, with a very short muzzle. Ears, small and set high on the head, are customarily cropped, though left natural in Great Britain. Tail, too, is customarily docked to about one-third. The Brussels stands 7–8 inches tall and is not to exceed 12 pounds. The rough variety can be reddish brown, black and reddish brown mixed, black with uni-

More than a spaniel, the Brittany epitomizes the all-around hunter's companion; he is both smart and people-loving.

Sedentary and content, the Bulldog happily snoozes with a young companion. This ancient English dog has an onslaught of admirers who love him for the easygoing Bully he is.

form reddish brown markings, or solid black. Black is not allowed for the smooth.

Essentially a one-person Griffon, the breed shuns too much affection and being mistaken for a lap dog (apparently it had its own seat in the cab). The dog requires only periodic stripping and doesn't mind skipping a walk or two.

BULLDOG

Descended from the fierce animal-baiting mastiffs of Europe long ago, the Bulldog breed has been gradually modified over the years to its present, highly refined type. Of medium size and smooth coat, the Bulldog is constructed of heavy bone, presenting a thick-set, low-slung appearance. Head is mas-

sive, accentuated by his short muzzle and small, high-set ears, never cropped. Chest, very broad, deep and full. Tail, always short, may be either straight or screw but never curled. Colors include red and other brindles, solid white, red-fawn or yellow, and piebald.

Today's Bulldog suffers from the exaggerated features that distinguish it from all other dogs. These are sweet, gentle, harmless companion animals who quickly win over their keepers. Breeding, whelping, respiration, and drooling should be considered by interested parties. Despite all his shortcomings, the Bulldog continues to maintain a healthy following. Discipline is essential, or else your adolescent may attempt bullying the family around.

BULLMASTIFF

Once named the "Gamekeeper's Night Dog," the Bullmastiff was bred for size, strength and fearlessness. The head is very large and broad, with the muzzle broad and deep. Characteristic facial wrinkles and flews complete the mastiffy appearance. Chest is broad and deep, and body overall is substantial and suggestive of great power. Weight, 110–130 pounds; height, 25–27 inches. Coat is short and smooth. Possible colors are red, fawn, and brindle, all with a black mask.

A rather mellow mollosser who does well in a home environment, given proper space and outdoor time. One of few breeds developed expressly for guard work, the Bullmastiff is a strong, loyal animal with natural protective instincts. Movement is of utmost importance in selecting a Bully—observe the parents, since puppies are typically awkward. Breeding often presents difficulties in certain oversized lines.

BULL TERRIER

Englishman James Hinks, father of the breed, crossed various game

A manly choice, the Bull Terrier makes a nifty house dog and is the smallest of the working guard-dog breeds.

bulldogs and plucky terriers in the 1850s to create, to his standards, the finest bull-and-terrier dog ever. The Bull Terrier today is most distinctive for his egg-shaped head and well-rounded body. The oval head is adorned with small, thin, closely placed ears and well-sunken dark eyes. Coat should be short, flat, and harsh to the touch. Color is broken down into two varieties: White, with markings only on the head; and Colored, brindle preferred. The Bull Terrier stands 21–22 inches tall and weighs 52–62 pounds.

A breed whose popularity has ebbed and flowed historically, the Bull Terrier enjoys high popularity for his matchless macho appeal and dashing, if not dapper, looks. More tolerant of other pets, even cats, than other bull-and-terrier breeds, the Bull Terrier does well but needs consistent training. Never underestimate the power of a BT, despite his moderate size.

CAIRN TERRIER

Of hardy Scotch stock, the Cairn Terrier was bred to bolt the fox, the otter, and other vermin. Necessarily scrappy and tough, this ten-inch terrier sports a rough and wiry weather-resistant jacket that should be kept in its natural state. Head is broad; eyes, protected by shaggy eyebrows, are hazel to dark hazel in color. Ears are small, pointed, and

The Cairn Terrier is renowned as a children's breed. Today he is a popular show dog and family pet in America and England.

carried erect. Tail, carried proudly, should not curl. Any color except white can be shown, with dark ears, muzzle and tail tip the norm.

Lifting the spirits of owners for countless generations, the Cairn Terrier is the pal of the canine world. Although the breed is more pet-oriented than most other working terriers, the Cairn's instinct to dig is hardly dormant. In Britain, the breed ranks among the most popular, though the U.S. has surprisingly fewer.

CARDIGAN WELSH CORGI

The low-to-the-ground Cardi stems from very old stock (tracing to 1200 B.C.) and has been used for centuries to herd livestock by nipping its heels, to which task his short legs and elongated body suit him perfectly. He is mostly distinguished from his stumpy-tailed cousin, the Pembroke, by a full fox-like tail. His head, too, is described as fox-like, and the erect ears are large in proportion to his overall size. Coat can be short or medium, and always of a hard texture. Color can be any, with or without white markings.

Cardigans, like the sweaters of the same name, are classics and fit most anyone handsomely. The tailed of the Corgis of Wales, this dog possesses much esteem and willingness to become involved. The breed's herding instincts are still somewhat pronounced, which leads the dogs to nip at the heels of children who unknowingly (and adults who knowingly) act like unruly cattle. A friendly outgoing dog that makes a long-lived and handy-sized companion.

An up-and-coming miniature breed in the States, Cavalier King Charles Spaniels sparkle as apartment dogs: these are typically one-person dogs with an abundance of spunk and charisma.

CAVALIER KING CHARLES SPANIEL

The modern Cavalier started in the 1920s as a reborn Blenheim Spaniel of the old type—the longer-headed toy spaniels captured in nineteenth-century paintings. He is a well-balanced dog offering a soft and gentle appearance. The long ears are adorned with plentiful feather. Tail may be left natural or docked by no more than one-third. Coat, long but never curly, is silky in texture. Four colors occur: black and tan; ruby (a rich red); Blenheim (rich chestnut markings on a white background); and tricolor (black and white with tan markings).

There truly is no breed quite like the Cavalier, and the British attest to this stout-heartedly. Americans, this time, are slow to catch on, but are doing so steadily. The Cav is a charming miniature—not a toy dog. The coat is luxurious but doesn't need excessive care. Apartments are ideal living space for the Cav.

CHESAPEAKE BAY RETRIEVER

The Chessie was born on the shores of the Chesapeake Bay, and he bloomed into a duck hunter par excellence. His substantial frame and broad facial construction provide great power in the workplace, and his thick, coarse, moderately short coat allows excellent protection from the elements, without being a hindrance in icy waters. Tail is rather long and tapering. A color called "dead grass" is most desir-

Chesapeake Bay Retrievers are active and very trainable. These professional hunting dogs must be kept busy to remain happy.

able, though any color from liver to hay is acceptable.

The kids' dog, the Chesapeake is the top! While the breed maintains strong hunting instincts and is an excellent water-gamesman, it loves the family and is affectionate in a "golden" way. Exercise needs are substantial but not as rigorous as one might suspect. The upperhand should be asserted early since the Chesapeake has a strong mind and ducky ideas of its own.

Chihuahuas are portable and industrious: gentle handling is required.

and travel but are limited as knock-about clowns. Personalities are often refreshing, though a certain yappiness might be expected. True indoor dogs for older people, Chihuahuas are adaptable and surprisingly hardy if well kept.

CHIHUAHUA

This apple-headed tot of a toy holds the distinction of being the smallest of all dog breeds. Weighing only 1–6 pounds, the Chihuahua stands proudly, revealing his "saucy" expression. In general having terrier-like qualities, his other distinctions include his well-rounded head, accentuated by lean cheeks and moderately short nose; large, erectly carried ears; and moderately long "sickle-shaped" tail. Two coat varieties exist: the smooth (i.e., short) and the long; both are soft in texture.

If you need a dog as a jogging and hiking companion, the Chihuahua is not it. Intense exercise can kill a Chihuahua, though they'll happily backpack (inside the pack, of course). They enjoy companionship

CHINESE CRESTED

Unabashed and unbashful, this hairless dog stands a proud 12–13 inches tall at most, and is concealed only on the head, tail, and feet with a crest, plume, and socks, respectively. A coated variety, known as the Powderpuff, also exists, and is identical in type, except for the longish, silky double coat. Skin color can range from pink to black, mahogany, blue, lavender, or copper; and it can be solid or spotted. The coated variety can be any color or combination of colors.

An open-minded, warm-hearted owner may consider the Chinese Crested, the most recognizable of the world's naked canine wonders. These dogs require much from their owners, as their lack of a coat presents special skin care, and the sun must be avoided. Additionally breeding hairless dogs differs from breeding coated dogs, and inexperienced persons are strongly discouraged. The breed's temperament is very dog-like and outgoing, quite normal and gay in every respect and more than a little endearing.

CHOW CHOW

Hailed as a great and ancient lord of China, the stalwart Chow Chow impresses one immediately with his massive, powerful appearance. The Chow Chow is of strong and muscular construction, accentuated by a massive head and scowling expression. Ears are small, rounded at the tip, and stiffly carried; the tongue is a distinctive blue-black color. Two coat types exist: the long, which is straight, off-standish, and, of course, long; and the smooth,

which is shorter and more plush.

The Chow Chow seduces many new dog owners with its alluring appearance and noble personality. No cowardly lion, the Chow is quite jealous and aloof with strangers, and frequently is not recommended for families with children. Discipline potentially presents a problem, as with many Oriental dogs, their intelligence precludes instinctive submission. The Rough Chow requires periodic grooming though is self-maintaining to a fair extent.

CLUMBER SPANIEL

Distinguished from his fellow spaniel relations by his thick-set, heavy, and low-to-the-ground construction, the Clumber was bred to

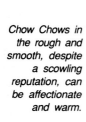

Chow Chows in the rough and smooth, despite a scowling reputation, can be affectionate and warm.

hunt slowly and methodically on grounds abundant in game. His massive head, heavy brow, and rather large, triangular ears offer a unique expression. Flews are very apparent. Legs are large-boned and short, and the tail is customarily docked. Clumbers are primarily col-

COCKER SPANIEL, AMERICAN

The ever-popular, ever-jubilant Cocker sweeps his audience with a sturdy compact build and pleasant, intelligent expression. His well-rounded head bears full, round eyes, clearly defined eyebrows and long feathered ears. Tail is customarily

Cocker Spaniels bask in the sun of popularity—well-deserved recognition of their merry and adaptable ways.

ored in white, with lemon or orange markings; the more white, the better. The Clumber stands 17–20 inches, and weighs 55–85 pounds.

Too many sportsmen overlook the Clumber. Admittedly not a tall dog, the Clumber Spaniel never ceases to delight his very devoted followers. The breed mistakenly has the reputation of being a lethargic, cumbersome animal—not true at all. This is an energetic and active dog that loves the hunt and his family equally!

docked. Coat is abundant, long and silky, with feathering on chest, stomach, and legs. Among the smallest of still functional gundogs, the Cocker stands 15 inches at most and weighs between 24–28 pounds. Coat color can be any solid color or particolor, including tricolor.

Epitomizing the dog's desire to please, the Cocker Spaniel has it all! The breed's disposition, according to the cries of many thousands of owners, is second to none. He is obedient and handsome and cute, easy to get along with, and adaptable to anyone's lifestyle (no matter how peculiar or mundane). As a general rule, buyers must be especially cautious when approaching sellers of a breed this popular.

COCKER SPANIEL, ENGLISH

Merry and proud, this derivative of the oldest land spaniels is both handsome and keenly intelligent. Standing 15–17 inches tall, he possesses a balanced, strongly constructed body and perfectly proportioned head. His distinctive muzzle should be square and blend harmoniously into the skull. Ears are long and well feathered; tail is customarily docked. The coat is short and smooth on the head, medium-length on the body, with abundant feathering on the ears, chest, abdomen and legs. Color can be solid, or in a broken pattern with white; roaning often occurs.

Slightly larger than his American brother, the Cocker Spaniel of England is merry by definition. The breed bonds strongly to its owners and may be envious of affection wasted on children. Exercise time helps to channel this little dog's abundant energy. Grooming parlor visits every few months keep the Cocker looking his finest.

The familiar Collie resonates the adage of "man's best friend."

COLLIE

Descended from a long line of fine Scotch herding dogs, the Collie has long impressed fanciers with its unique and beautiful appearance. Two coat varieties exist: the more

Curly-Coated Retriever

Less common than most other retrievers, the Curly-Coated has been used by hunters for generations.

common Rough, adorned with a long, dense coat; and the Smooth, protected by a short, smooth coat. The Collie is distinctive for his long, narrow head, resembling a blunt clean wedge. The expressive eyes are considered of great importance. Ears, small, carried semi-erect. Colors include sable and white, tricolor, and blue merle. Height: 22–26 inches. Weight: 50–75 pounds.

For any child (or adult) growing up with a television, the Collie is a common sight, and represents the epitome of intelligence and devotion to its master. The breed has been employed on farms but the show ring is the Collie's true arena. Not since Will Rogers has a more perfect showman been encoun-

tered. The coat of the Rough requires constant attention. Affectionate and giving, the Collie is the choice of many dog people with enough room in his home and heart.

CURLY-COATED RETRIEVER
Bred specifically to retrieve game in the water, this hardy worker stands 25–27 inches tall, weighs 70–80 pounds, and is most distinctive for his close, crisp curls, which are small in size and cover his entire body, excepting the face. This coat is exceptionally waterproof and labeled "self-drying." He is a squarely built and very muscular dog, with a deep chest and long, well-proportioned head. Two colors occur: solid black and solid liver.

A water dog that excels in both retrieving and ground hunting, the Curly Coated is not a common retriever to find. Its talents are plenty, though the breed is not recommended for non-hunters. Show-dog people have experienced much success with the breed, as it is obedient and willing to please.

DACHSHUND
The uniquely long and low-to-the-ground construction of the Dachs-

hund was specifically bred for through the centuries to adapt this canine to following badger and other game right into their dens. Two varieties, divided by size, exist: the Miniature, weighing less than nine pounds; and the Standard, weighing 15–25 pounds. Additionally, there are three coat varieties: the smooth, having a short, thick, shining coat; the wirehaired, with a short, thick, rough and hard coat; and the longhaired, possessing a long, silky coat, like a setter's. All varieties can be one-colored, two-colored, or dappled, which is a clear ground with dark irregular patches.

Although a competent sportsman, the Dachshund of today excels as a companion and show animal. Owners are reminded of the dog's potential back difficulties and strongly urged to discourage their dogs from jumping (and Dachsies like to jump!). These dogs are happiest when they are active and

The longhaired Standard Dachshund stands out as one of the most popular of varieties.

attended to. Quite bold and daring, the Dachshund in either size is both a hound and a terrier of strong instinct.

DALMATIAN

This indisputably ancient breed possesses a sturdy, symmetrical construction and keen intelligence that has adapted it to a multitude of uses by man. Standing a moderate 19–23 inches tall and weighing 50–55 pounds, the spotted Dalmatian possesses a short, hard, dense coat that offers considerable protection. His distinctive color pattern consists of a pure white base with well-defined (not blotchy) black or liver spots.

Sensitive and sensible, the Dalmatian today is enjoying a new

Dandie Dinmont Terrier

Unmistakable in appearance and elegance, the Dalmatian is active and inquisitive.

resurgence of popularity. These dogs are unique as their spots and cannot be clumped together under any broad grouping. Their bird-dog instincts are strong and they require much exercise. Puppies are born pure white and slowly develop their spots. Begin training early and make the Dalmatian know he is loved and that you know he is there.

DANDIE DINMONT TERRIER

This short-legged, long bodied terrier shares stock with such hardy canines as the Lakeland and Bedlington Terriers. The Dandie, however, standing 8–11 inches tall, was bred specially to bolt the badger and otter. His crisp mixture of hard and soft hair offers protection and a unique look. The coat is two inches long and should never be wiry. Head is proportionately large with a full topknot. Tail, rather short. Two spicy colors are available: pepper (ranging from dark bluish black to light silvery gray) and mustard (ranging from reddish brown to pale fawn).

A snappy, sincere and serene dog about the house, the Dandie offers owners a charming purebred companion. Its easycare jacket requires occassional plucking. As far as small terriers go, the breed is one of the most distinctive and attractive. Exercise keeps the dandy well-toned, and many don't take too well to crate-training. Show-ring Dandies do dandy though they do need a run to the salon to fix their hair-dos and to tidy up.

DOBERMAN PINSCHER

A miraculous concoction of canines, the lean and powerful Dobie presents the image of being chiseled from steel. The breed stands 24–28 inches and weighs a deceptive 66–88 solid pounds. The short, sleek coat hides no rippling muscle or substantial bone. Head, long and clean, resembling a blunt wedge. Ears are either cropped and carried erect, or uncropped and carried drop. Tail, customarily docked to first or second joint. Color can be a solid ground of black, red, blue, or fawn, all with tan markings.

Surely the breed's decline in popularity in the U.S. is a positive thing for prospective American owners. The Doberman Pinscher is a more reliable and biddable guard dog today than he was during the rage of his popularity. The Doberman Pinscher promises its owner protection and devotion; early socialization helps ensure the dog's proper development, not to be complicated by ear-cropping, which, of course, British fanciers do not tolerate.

ENGLISH SETTER

The ideal coupling of elegance and utility has made the English Setter a favorite for centuries. Standing 24–25 inches tall, he is adorned with a fairly long flat coat, with feathering on the legs, tail, and underbody. The characteristic head is long and lean, with a long square muzzle. He is a very balanced, symmetrical dog weighing 40–70 pounds. Colors include a tricolor and blue, lemon, liver and orange, often with ticking against white.

Ideally the English Setter is a very attractive, very athletic dog. Presently, however, you may find either beautiful uninspired hunters or unrefined Olympiads—rarely do the twain meet. Fortunately breeders

A functional and stylish guard dog, the Doberman Pinscher was developed specifically for protection work. Puppies intended for such work should be properly reared.

have begun reemphasizing working abilities in show lines, so the beauties may soon acquire working prowess yet. The show dog's long hair requires some regular care to avoid matting, and the hunter's coat should be checked for burs routinely.

ENGLISH SPRINGER SPANIEL

Sprightly and springy, this neat and compact spaniel sports a moderately long and glossy coat, with feathering on the legs, ears, chest and underbody; a strong but refined head, and a docked tail. The leggiest of land spaniels, he is an exceptionally symmetrical and balanced dog, combining beauty and utility. He stands a moderate 19–20 inches tall and weighs 49–55 pounds. Coat colors include black and white, liver and white, and black or liver tricolor.

Popular as a show dog and companion, the English Springer is traditionally a bird dog and its hunting urges are easily tapped. Few dogs can offer the brains and the beauty of the Springer, nor does there exist a more pleasant and respect-worthy companion animal with whom to share your home. Unless socialized to small children, Springers may prefer not to spend time with young folk.

ENGLISH TOY SPANIEL

Retaining many fine spaniel characteristics in a 9–12-pound dog, the Toy Spaniel was created by the best

A beauty of a hunting dog, the English Springer Spaniel solicits new fanciers with his soulful eyes and loving expression.

The Finnish Spitz, quite new to the American dog scene, is smart looking and thinking.

breeding efforts of Japan, Spain, and England. Standing only 10 inches tall, this toy dog is noted for its well-domed skull; short, well-turned-up nose; and long, heavily feathered ears. Body should be strong, with substantial legs, short broad back and chest. Four color varieties occur: the King Charles, a black and tan; the ruby, a solid chestnut red; the Blenheim, a red and white; and the Prince Charles, a tricolor.

Elderly folk with limited living space have found the English Toy Spaniel a capital delight! These are cheerful and reliable lap chums who take their role as companion with near-comic seriousness. While the demands on an owner are few, the coat, long ears, and eyes should be regularly attended to. Generally, the breed enjoys quality time with its owner.

FIELD SPANIEL

At one time a very heavy, long, and low-set dog, the Field Spaniel today is a well-balanced, active and enduring dog who stands 18 inches tall and weighs 35–50 pounds. He is a classically unexaggerated spaniel type, with well-developed head and long muzzle. Coat is moderate in length, lying flat or slightly wavy, with feathering on legs, ears, and belly. Tail is customarily docked. Color can be black, liver, golden liver, and red, with or without tan markings; white markings are discouraged.

A sensible choice for the hunter, this spaniel performs admirably on the field, as its name surely conveys. The Field Spaniel does not often make his way into pet-only homes, as does the smaller Cocker. The breed is regarded with affection by those who know and work him.

FINNISH SPITZ

This old Finnish native holds great respect in his homeland as a fine hunter and companion. Attractively coated in dense, off-standish hair, fairly short in length, the Finnish Spitz occurs in chestnut red to pale red-gold color, with all puppies born brown. Head is broad across the top, with a tapering muzzle and erect triangular ears. Tail is carried loosely curled over the back. Height: 15.5–20 inches. Weight: 25–30 pounds.

A purebred of charm and keen intelligence, the Finsky enchants newcomers to the breed by its sensitivity and sharp looks. A sure joy of the spitz breeds guarantees that each dog will have a strong personality all his own. In Finland the breed continues to work on birds, though in the U.S. and Britain, more emphasis has been placed on compatibility with home and show. Keep in mind the Finsky can bark, and enjoys it, you bet!

FLAT-COATED RETRIEVER

Though never attaining the enormous popularity of his Golden or Labrador cousins, this no-nonsense gundog was "The Retriever" of Great Britain during the late 1800s. He stand 22–23 inches tall and weighs a solid 60–70 pounds. His coat, either solid black or solid liver, is of moderate length, density and fullness; it has a natural high luster. As indicated in the name, the straight coat should lie flat to the body. Ears, chest, back of forelegs and thighs, and underside of tail are well feathered.

Forever a puppy, the Flat-Coat relates well to his keepers and performs devotedly in the worst conditions for his master. This remarkably balanced dog delivers considerable gains to the hunter that employs him, as his talents in the field are plush. The coat requires little in terms of care.

FOXHOUNDS, AMERICAN/ ENGLISH

Selective breeding on two different sides of the Atlantic has resulted in two similar though slightly different dogs of like ancestry. The American Foxhound stands 21–25 inches, while the slightly larger English stands 23–27 inches. The American coat is close, hard, not too short; the English dog's coat, very short and hard. All hound colors acceptable on the American, but blue is not allowed on the English. Both are hot-nosed, enduring hounds.

The Foxhound breeds of America and England are principally employed by hunters and farmers who concentrate on fox hunting in small numbers or in packs, or on drag races. These are biddable, trusting animals who love children and require a great deal of exercise. Not recommended to non-sportsman types.

FOX TERRIERS, SMOOTH/WIRE
The Smooth and Wire Fox Terriers, similar except for coat type, keep separate breed status. The older wire type sports a hard, wiry, very dense jacket. The smooth type wears a short, hard but also very dense coat. On both breeds white should predominate; otherwise, markings not important, provided that they are not brindle, red or liver. These dogs are substantially boned and very strong, standing 15.5 inches tall and weighing 16–18 pounds. Balance is considered strongly.

Proverbial canines, the Fox Terriers in both coats are delightful, centerstage companions. Small enough to fit into most any lifestyle, though far too large to overlook, the breeds retain strong personalities as well as hunting instincts, which can be channeled towards a number of chores. Active adults and polite children form the Fox Terrier's preferred family. Wire Foxes need grooming parlor treatment to meet their show-ring ideal.

FRENCH BULLDOG
This bantamized bulldog with a distinctly French twist bears large "bat ears" and large round eyes upon his massive, square head. Body is short and rounded. Legs,

Dominant and endearing, the Wire Fox Terrier soars as a choice companion and a classic showman. Owners have long found the Fox Terriers to be the most adaptable and outgoing of the terrier breeds.

The French Bulldog, or Frenchie, is a delightful and winning small dog.

straight and stout, are also short. The short tail, like the English Bulldog's, can be either straight or screw, but never curled. Height: 12 inches. Height: two classes; lightweight, under 22 pounds; heavyweight, 22–28 pounds. Coat is short and smooth. Color can be brindle, fawn, with or without white markings; piebald or white.

A find for any dog lover, the French Bulldog is a unique breed that offers an alert, intelligent dog of a dog in a smallish package. Sometimes mistaken for a toy dog, the Frenchie is a quaint little gentleman who can serve handsomely as a watchdog and is an active, fun pet that enjoys children and adults. Seniors have also found this easycare buddy ideal for adopting.

GERMAN SHEPHERD DOG

Among the most highly esteemed and most popular dogs ever to bark, the German Shepherd Dog maintains a strong following throughout the world. He stands a proud 22–26 inches and weighs a strong 75–95 pounds. A well-balanced animal, slightly longer than tall, he possesses a substantial body, with deep chest, muscular thighs, and solid limbs. Head, cleanly chiseled, bears large, erect ears. Coat, moderately short but with a dense undercoat, occurs in black and tan, sable, and all black.

Potential owners of the German Shepherd need not be converted. The advantages and appeal of the breed are easily evidenced: a protection dog with super-canine smarts, an even-tempered demeanor, and a loving, playful outlook on life. German Shepherds need attention and should not be taken for granted. Socialization and exercise are musts. These dogs play rough and must be supervised around young children.

GERMAN SHORTHAIRED POINTER

German huntsmen blended the best of pointers, foxhounds, and tracking dogs to create the German Shorthair, a versatile and dedicated hunter. Once heavy, long-eared and otherwise more houndy, the well-balanced breed today stands a lean 23–25 inches, weighing 55–70 pounds. Head is clean, neither light nor heavy; ears, broad, lie flat. Tail

The German Shepherd Dog continues to top the list of purebred dogs.

is docked to two-fifths. Coat is short, thick, and rough to the touch. Color can be solid liver, or any combination of liver and white, with or without ticking.

This energetic, affectionate dog can be the ideal pet for any owner who understands how this talented German sportsman ticks. His hunting needs should be met—weekend outings at least will help satiate his craving—plus a lot of exercise to help work off his terrific energy. A long-lived, easycare dog with great potential around children.

GERMAN WIREHAIRED POINTER

The gruff and grandfatherly German Wirehair represents a blend of some of the finest hunting dogs in Germany. Produced in the late 1800s as a universal hunter, the German Wirehair stands a rugged 24–26 inches tall and weighs 60–70 pounds. His all-protective harsh wiry coat consists of a flat outer coat, with heavy beard and eye brows, and dense undercoat. Color can be solid

The German Shorthaired Pointer has a fraternity of staunch supporters who profess that this is the most accomplished of all the world's hunting dogs.

liver or any combination of liver and white. In Europe, black, in any combination with white, is also an accepted color.

An intelligent, sensitive dog, the German Wirehaired Pointer is a proven working dog that requires consistent training and a big time commitment. As pets these dogs are entertaining and always playful. Many breeders contend that they are more at home in an outdoor kennel than in the home. Grooming is not terribly demanding but necessary.

GIANT SCHNAUZER

Truly an impressive dog, this giant of a Schnauzer traces to the fear-

Golden Retriever

less cattle-droving butcher dogs of Germany. He is remarkably similar in appearance to the smaller Schnauzer types, but in sheer size and power, there is no comparison. The Giant stands 23–27.5 inches and weighs 70–77 pounds. His hard bristly coat is medium in length with a woolly undercoat. Colors are solid black or pepper and salt. Ears are customarily cropped, standing erect; and tail is normally docked short.

A dog who waited patiently for its time to come (or return), the breed today is a Schnauzer of many trades. The Giant needs a home with large grounds, an owner with much time to spend on grooming and exercise, and a family that needs protection and a lot of love. The dog's coat has the tendency to go soft if not properly attended, so owners must respect this important long-time breed trait.

GOLDEN RETRIEVER

Renowned for his obedience and trainability, the Golden Retriever has captured the hearts of dog lovers in general with his beauty, symmetry, and loving nature. The Golden stands 21.5–24 inches tall and is adorned with a medium-length dense coat that lies flat to the body; the hair itself may be flat or wavy; moderate feathering on back of forelegs and underbody; heavier on the neck, back of thighs, and underside of tail. Color is a rich golden of various shades and an invariable lustrous sheen.

An absolutely grand choice for the dog owner and consistently a

Prominent for his versatility and trainability, the Giant Schnauzer is a good big-dog option, with many and varied talents.

The Golden Retriever cannot be easily resisted by the family man. Unqualified affection and good looks define the Golden breed, and it makes a wonderful choice for the kids.

popular one, the Golden Retriever is arguably the most handsome gundog, the most obedient worker and the loyalest, lovingest, kindest dog any owner could dream of. The virtues of the breed are well known and well deserved. The coat requires a good brushing every couple days and field work and exercise are recommended by breeders today to keep the dog active and responsive.

GORDON SETTER

He is an elegant, intelligent, and undeniably good birding dog with the character to make him an excel-

lent pet dog as well. Standing 23–27 inches tall and weighing 45–80 pounds, the Gordon Setter is adorned with a moderately long straight or slightly wavy coat that lies flat to the body, accentuated by long feathering on the ears, chest, underbody, tail and backs of legs. Ears, carried down, are fairly large. Tail is moderately short. Color is invariably black with tan markings.

Despite the allure of this attractive dog, the Gordon Setter still remains a dynamic working bird dog. The breed's instincts are thankfully intact and pet owners discover that the dogs make better pets if worked and trialed. They are generally clean and well mannered, but should not be confined indoors lest they become high-strung and unhappy.

A spectacular, sinewy example of the Great Dane. Not the breed for everyone, the Dane needs an active and confident keeper.

GREAT DANE

Nicknamed the Apollo of the dog world, the Great Dane is one of the tallest of all breeds, standing at least 28–32 inches tall. Bred originally to hunt the boar, this powerful canine weighs a substantial 100 pounds or more. Head is long, narrow, and finely chiseled. Chest is broad, deep, and well muscled. The tapering tail is never docked. Ears are either cropped and carried erect, or left natural and carried folded. Color can be brindle, fawn, blue, black, or harlequin (pure white base with black patches).

A big dog with a big appetite, the Great Dane cannot survive on a budget, in a condo, or without sufficient entertainment. Grooming needs are few, though the need for vigorous exercise makes up for gained time. Despite his grand size, the dog is not recommended as a man-halting guard dog since its temperament is too docile. Best suited for athletic owners who enjoy a dog who wants an active part in his lifestyle.

GREAT PYRENEES

Powerful and proud, the Great Pyr has been guarding flocks in his native France since at least 1000 B.C. Known as the Pyrenean Mountain Dog in Britain, he is a dog of great size and substance, good proportion and balance. Height: 25–32 inches. Weight: 90–140 pounds. His very abundant coat is medium to medium-long. Color is white, or white with patches of badger, wolf-gray, or pale yellow. These patches should occur only on the head, ears and base of tail.

Docility and sweetness incarnate,

Docile and steady, the Great Pyrenees needs property and family to oversee. The breed cannot be recommended for serious guard work, though his size is a substantial deterrent to those who don't know his mild manners.

this oversized Frenchman reigns as the ultimate estate dog. Although its days of guarding sheep seem far beyond the pet Pyr, the dog is generally protective of its family. Nonetheless, like the Great Dane, the dog is too mild and non-aggressive to function as a guard dog. Grooming requirements cannot be underestimated and shedding can be abundant.

GREYHOUND

He is aerodynamic and strongly constructed, able to reach great speeds in seemingly effortless strides: the Greyhound is the epitome of the running hound. Standing 27–30 inches tall, he weighs a deceiving 60–70 solidly muscled pounds. Limbs, long and sinewy, support a lithe body, marked by very deep chest and strong abdominal tuck-up. Head is long and well chiseled. Ears are small and described as rose-shaped. Tail is long and tapering. Coat, short and smooth, can be any color.

Not suited to family pets unless a rigorous exercise regimen can be instituted, the Greyhound can be a well-balanced, sleek companion animal. Coursing events and races help guarantee the proper development of this athlete's psyche. The dogs are potentially "jumpy," so children or nervous adults may not be appropriate company for the Greyhound. Retired racing Greyhounds often find their ways to farms and ranches where they are proficient rodent-detectors.

Greyhound puppy enjoying the sights and scents of its new world.

HARRIER

To develop a medium-sized pack-hound, British hunters of centuries past crossed heavy hounds with smaller, lighter hounds, such as the Beagle. The result was the Harrier, a breed that much resembles a small foxhound in type, standing 19–22 inches and weighing a strong 48–60 pounds. He is an active and well-balanced dog of sound quality and strong instinct. Coat is short, coarse and hard. Any hound color is acceptable.

A good-sized dog, the Harrier can make a remarkable pet and hunting dog. Socialization and proper consistent training are required to bring about the desired temperament. Stubbornness is not unknown, typical of intelligent breeds of dog. Exercising this hard-running hound goes without saying. The breed unfortunately suffers from low registration numbers and is not commonly seen at dog shows.

IBIZAN HOUND

An ancient dog tracing back some 30 centuries before Christ, this native Spaniard possesses the long legs and lithe, graceful construction that identify him immediately as a swift running hound. He stands 22.5–27.5 inches tall and weighs a lean 42–55 pounds. Ears are large and upstanding. Tail is long and tapering. Two coat types exist: shorthaired, being short, close-lying, and hard; and wirehaired, being hard, coarse, and 1–3 inches long. Color can be solid red, white or tawny; or white with either red or tawny.

A unique animal, the Ibizan Hound, with its prominent, supersonic ears, makes a sleek companion and is remarkably trainable to many tasks. This is a tall dog that requires a lot of running. Health problems are fairly uncommon though exposure to extreme cold is not wise. Owners find these dogs more sensitive than many other sighthounds, though independence remains of the essence.

IRISH SETTER

The Irish Setter is prized for his aristocratic, substantial yet elegant construction. Attractive yet functional, this regal bird dog sports an attractive coat of moderately long straight hair that lies flat to the body. Long feathering adorns the ears, back of legs, belly and chest. His distinctive color is described as mahogany or rich chestnut red. Head is long and lean; ears, long and end in a neat fold. Body is fairly long; tail, moderately long and well feathered. Height: 23–27 inches. Weight: 60–70 pounds.

A sensitive, intelligent dog, the Irish Setter, always hailed for its good looks, is a sensible choice for a pet animal. The breed's talents are seemingly unlimited. Owners are warned that these are inventive, mentally active dogs who should not be left to improvise too long without supervision. Breeding stock is much improved over the past few generations, since the breed has survived its wave of popularity.

IRISH TERRIER

The Irish Terrier is a dog of speed, power, and endurance, and these qualities are clearly reflected in his balanced, symmetrical construction. Standing 18 inches tall, the Irish Terrier possesses a long, proportionate head, moderately long body, and strong, muscular legs. Ears are small and V-shaped, folded and dropping forward. The harsh, wiry

Introduced to the field at a young age, the Irish Setter can excel as a hunting dog, though most breed representatives today enjoy lives as pets and show dogs.

coat is dense but lies fairly close to the body. Color should be a whole-colored red, golden red, red wheaten or wheaten.

Decide the role of your Irish Terrier before he does! These are outgoing, game terriers who will not concede to lead training if not introduced at an early age. This is a smart-sized dog that fits well into any home and whose exercise requirements are happily modest. The wire coat does not require stripping, and dead-hair removal is not time-consuming.

IRISH WATER SPANIEL

This water dog first appeared in Ireland in the 1830s. His distinctive coat is composed of tight, crisp ringlets on the body, neck and tail, with

Irish Wolfhound

The Irish Water Spaniel is a sizable, multi-functional hunting dog with a novel look to him—water is his forte.

longer hair, loosely curled on the legs and top of the head; short smooth hair covers the face, and back of the legs. Height is 21–24 inches, and weight is between 45–65 pounds. The Irish Water Spaniel is a strongly built dog of rugged appearance and great intelligence. Color is always a solid liver, without any white markings.

A tractable, hard-working gundog, the Irish Water Spaniel has lakes and rivers of talents and is overflowing with personality. With strangers he is sensible, aloof. Training the dog for work is a cinch. Grooming is required and the breed is never clipped. The breed loves the attention of children but can be as ram-bunctious as the most untrained urchin.

IRISH WOLFHOUND

The tallest of the running hounds, this antique Irishman has coursed his native isle with strength, courage, and enthusiasm since well before the time of Christ. Ideally he stands 32–34 inches at the shoulder. Weight for females, at least 105 pounds; for males, 120 pounds. Head, neck, and back are substantially long; chest is deep; and overall appearance is commanding and majestic. Coat is rough, hard, and especially wiry and long over eyes and underjaw. Color can be gray, brindle, red, black, pure white, fawn, or any other color that appears in the Deerhound.

The horse of the canine species, the Irish Wolfhound has requirements that are obtrusively obvious. If you do not have a large yard and sufficient time to train the dog, keep thumbing through this book. Puppies (under one year) need special time daily to socialize and train, as dogs through adolescence are characteristically excitable and bouncy. As an adult, this skyscraper is quiet and biddable, a genuinely lovable breed.

ITALIAN GREYHOUND

Hailed as the first of the toy breeds, this miniature sighthound traces to

The tallest of all dogs, the Irish Wolfhound requires miles for running and plenty of time and nutrition.

ancestors found in the ancient tombs of Egypt. Standing 13–15 inches tall, he weighs in at six to eight pounds. Of classic running-hound type, the IG has a long, narrow, tapering head; medium-length, high-to-the-ground body; and long, well-muscled legs. Ears are small and carried back except when alert. Coat is short and smooth. Color can be all shades of fawn, red, mouse, blue, cream and white; black and tan is not allowed.

As easygoing, easycare home companion, the Italian Greyhound should not be mistaken for a spunkless, mouse-like, mouse-colored creature. Their temperament is kind and fun-loving. Their petite size and gentle natures evoke consideration and delicate care. So minimally coated, the breed is easily chilled and rough play with children is strongly advised against.

JACK RUSSELL TERRIER

During the mid-nineteenth century, Rev. Jack Russell crossed various fox-hunting terriers and feisty bull-and-terrier dogs to create a tough, leggier terrier that could follow a horsemen and bolt a fox that went to ground. In height, the JRT is 9–15 inches. Coat is rough and either very short and wiry or smooth. Color must be better than half white, with tricolor, brown or black marks.

Hardy, good-natured dogs, the Jack Russell Terriers epitomize a working farm terrier and a snappy family pet. The breed boasts a reputation for fearlessness and an irreverent sense of humor, despite their creator. Lifespans are promising, though the dogs must be supervised at all times, as they do not perceive danger or self-destruction.

JAPANESE CHIN

This ancient bantamized breed of the Orient strongly suggests spaniel ancestry. Once called the Japanese Spaniel, the Chin offers a dainty yet compact appearance. His head is large, with large eyes and small ears; muzzle is very short. Body is square, with a wide chest and small-boned legs. The breed is divided in two by weight: over seven pounds; and under seven pounds, the smaller the better. Coat is straight, long and profuse; abundant feathering adorns the ears, chest, thighs, tail, and especially the neck. Color can be black and white or red and white.

An indoor delight, the Japanese Chin has a centuries' old roster of

An attractive, feisty little dog, the Jack Russell Terrier corners the market on rodent clean-up and quality companionship.

Keep your Chin up! These Nipponese tots are playful and handy-sized handfuls—great miniatures for the human tots too.

good qualities. Unlike some other toy breeds, the Chin epitomizes the perfect houseguest. He is polite, quiet, undemanding, cordial to visitors, and willing to sit with and for the children. Owners must see to it that the Chin is treated with reciprocal consideration as he himself is but a tot.

KEESHOND

This Dutch variation of the ancient spitz-type dogs of the North is adorned with a profuse coat that forms a dense ruff around the neck, thick trousers on the hind legs, and heavy feathering on the forelegs. The coat is harsh, off-standing and straight overall. Head is wedge-shaped; ears small and erect; tail, moderately long, carried tightly curled over the back. Height: 17–19 inches. Weight: 55–66 pounds. Color is wolf-gray, with lighter shading on head and undersides, creating the typical spectacles around the eyes.

The family dog, the Keeshond is the perfect size for a pet, not so small to be squishable and not so large as to require half a county to exercise properly. The Keeshond thrives on the company of children, who are as rowdy and happy-go-lucky as he is. Ideally children who love their Keeshond will also learn to groom him, as tangles are to be expected if the coat is not attended.

breed must be shown in the rough (unclipped). Kerries are born black; during their transition phase they may exhibit a very dark blue, shades of brown, and mixtures of these, until they reach their mature gray-blue or blue-gray color.

Despite his convenient size, the Kerry Blue should not be confined to apartment life. Exercise helps keep the Kerry alert and bids away the

KERRY BLUE TERRIER

Of true "blue-collar" working derivation, the Kerry is an ideal sporting terrier, with a balanced, well-muscled construction. This centuries' old Irishman stands 17.5–19.5 inches and weighs 33–40 pounds. His profuse coat, soft, dense and wavy, is a most highly regarded feature. In his native Ireland, the

Kerry Blues are black at birth, but later acquire their classic blue coloration. As an adult, the Kerry is a medium-sized, quick-minded terrier.

blues. The dog may enjoy children but is not generally recommended as an ideal choice for a house full of children. Discipline is recommended to focus this headstrong dog's personality in a positive, desirable direction.

KOMONDOR

With corded coat and concrete courage, the Komondor has worked the fields of Europe for thousands of years. He exhumes a commanding appearance: his head, wide and of generous size; his chest, deep and powerful; his legs, well boned and muscular—all shrouded beneath his most distinctive dense, weather-resistant corded coat. His tassel-like cords occur naturally. Coat color is white, with gray, not pink, skin ideal. Height: males at least 25.5 inches; females at least 23.5 inches. Weight: 80–150 pounds.

A Komondor in a full coat of cords does not freeze outdoors, is protected from potential opponents, and makes a heck of a head-turner and conversation piece. The breed requires considerably special grooming, and bathing is an all-day affair. The dog is a leader and therefore needs firm guidance from puppyhood. Adult coats develop by two years of age; the puppy coat is curly and dense.

KUVASZ

From massive Tibetan dogs, the Kuvasz was developed centuries ago in Hungary, where he played the ever-present and intimidating role of guardian. Mellowed and reduced in size, the Kuvasz today still stands 26–30 inches tall, with dogs weighing between 100–115 pounds, and bitches 70–90 pounds. He is a solidly and proportionately built dog of notable working ability. Coat is medium coarse in texture, ranging from wavy to straight; medium length on the body, short on the head and paws; feathering adorns the rear of the forelegs, and a thick mane covers the neck, extending to the chest.

Too often overlooked in the crowd, the Kuvasz possesses good looks, good faith, and good potential to protect his family. This is a big dog that benefits from a solid, unexaggerated frame and keen intelligence. Indiscriminate with his affections and ideal for family life, the Kuvasz is a sensible choice for many persons and not too difficult to acquire.

No small undertaking, the Komondor is a strong-willed, thickly coated, big dog that requires an owner's all.

LABRADOR RETRIEVER

From Newfoundland, land of cold and coldwater sailing vessels, comes the Labrador Retriever. From native fishermen's dogs, the breed has been developed into a fine sporting and companion dog. Height: 21.5–24.5 inches. Weight: 55–75 pounds. He is strongly built, proportionately short and of good width. Coat is close fitting, short and dense; it is free of feather and very water resistant. The distinctive tail is described as an "otter tail," being short, very thick and tapering. Three colors occur: black, yellow, and chocolate.

An outdoorsman from the word go, the Labrador cannot resist the home life either. This is a flawless, adaptable family dog with an abundance of energy and affection; a dog who is both biddable and intelligent. Rough-housing with children and sprints on the beach are of the essence for this active and talented animal.

LAKELAND TERRIER

As suggested in his name, the Lakeland hails from England's Lake District—the landscape to Wordsworth's poetry and the most symmetrical of terrier breeds. Believed to be of the oldest extant working terrier type, the breed sports an array of colors, including blue, black, liver, black and tan, blue and tan, red, red grizzle, grizzle and tan, and wheaten. His coat is hard and wiry, with plentiful facial furnishings. Tail is customarily docked. Height: 13–15 inches. Weight: 17 pounds.

The Lakeland should not be regarded as a nippy terrier, though defending himself is not a problem. This moderate-sized dog is most amenable to the company of youths, as are most terriers.

Given to hard play and hands-on affection, the Labrador Retriever steadily ranks with the best of all possible dogs.

Their consistent and gay demeanor well suits them for a variety of homes.

LHASA APSO

Mysterious and long-isolated, Tibet gave birth to the Lhasa, a vigorous dog given as a "sacred" gift and believed to have special protective powers over homes. The Lhasa today wears a long, heavy, straight and hard coat; the head is covered in heavy furnishings that fall over the eyes; a beard is also present; the tail, carried well over the back, is heavily feathered. The breed occurs in many colors, including golden, sandy, grizzle, smoke, black, brown, white, and particolors. Height: 10–11 inches.

An abundance of off-standing fur and a royal disposition, the Lhasa Apso fits onto an owner's lap—momentarily. This little dog is not lap-dog material and does not relish coddling, though occasional cuddling is good for his Buddhist soul. The coat requires constant care in order to maintain the proper appearance. Despite his big-dog outlook, a lot of exercise is not required for muscle tone.

MALTESE

The majestic Maltese, like his bichon relatives, resulted from thousands of years of selective breeding that bantamized and blended Poodles, water dogs, and other well-coated sporting types. Weighing less than seven pounds, this toy breed is adorned completely with a long, silky

The luxuriant coat of the Maltese is this angel's trademark—this little dog can really tangle his owner up with love and admiration.

coat. Ideally he is pure white. The tail is heavily feathered (a "plume") and carried over the back.

Since the initial attraction to the Maltese is his coat, let us warn you that it does not maintain itself! This dog requires long hours of brushing and therefore daily attention is not optional. He is a sweet, mild-mannered dog who is surprisingly active and doesn't milk the toy dog windowseat.

An uncommon black-and-tan darling, the erect-eared Manchester Terrier is a lively, longlived dog that is choice for apartment dwellers.

MANCHESTER TERRIERS, STANDARD AND TOY

During the 1500s, and even before, black and tan terriers earned their keep in England by slaying vermin by the score. From these hardy, hard-bitten dogs resulted two modern breeds, divided by size: the Manchester Terrier and the Toy Manchester Terrier. Refined and cultured, the Manchesters of today possess an elegant, clean appearance, marked by a compact body; a long, flat and narrow skull; and a short, tapering tail. Ears of the Toy are of moderate size and must not be cropped; ears of the Standard are small and may be cropped. The smooth, short coat lies close to the body and bears a natural gloss. Color invariably black and tan (mahogany). Size: Toy, 7–12 pounds; Standard, either 12–16 pounds, or 16–22 pounds.

Very similar dogs in appearance, the Manchester Terriers are surprisingly alike as pets too. The Standard and Toy varieties are easycare animals and enjoy time indoors. The Standard does require time outdoors but does not have excessive energy. The Toy fends more hardily than the average tiny house dog and enjoys playing. These are essentially longlived, loyal companion animals.

MASTIFF

This canine powerhouse descends from some of the oldest and most battle-hardened of dogs, tracing back thousands of years before Christ. Though his temperament has mellowed, the Mastiff has retained great size and strength, standing 27.5–30 inches tall and weighing 175–190 pounds or more. His distinctive skull is very broad; muzzle, short, broad and blunt; ears small, lying flat. Body is very substantial; with deep, wide chest and straight, powerful back. Coat is short, dense, and moderately coarse. Color can be apricot, silver fawn, or dark fawn-brindle, all with dark muzzle, ears and nose.

This is a giant of a dog and arguably the heaviest in the world! The Mastiff offers the right owner a lot of dog but owners must approach the purchase of a Mastiff with utter caution. These are dogs full of docility, sweetness and personality, and are very habit-oriented. Transplanting a Mastiff from one home to another is rarely successful so, with due respect to the dogs, owners must carefully consider this breed. Exercise needs are not overwhelming but owners must make a point of

The mountain-like Mastiff is a lot of dog to train, feed and climb. Well-reared Mastiffs are reliable and gentle with children, and make unbudgeable babysitters.

walking the dog regularly or else the laziness thickens. A fine guard dog and a reliable companion to boot. A large fenced-in yard should be a qualification for ownership.

MINIATURE PINSCHER

Popularly known as "king of the toys," the MinPin is a sturdy and compact dog of high spirit and animation. To call him a Mini Doberman is taxingly insulting, as his purebred ancestry dates back far before that of the Dobe. The MinPin is an exceedingly well-balanced dog, with a narrow tapering head and clean, muscular body in perfect proportion. Ears are erect, and may be cropped or uncropped. Tail, customarily docked. Coat is smooth

Miniature Schnauzer

and short. Color can be clear red, stag red (red with intermingling of black hairs), or black and tan. Height: 10–12.5 inches.

This well-rounded, attractive toy dog is surely a joy to own. The Miniature Pinscher is a confident, outgoing dog that needs but one person to love and for whom to perform. The MinPin's antics delight adults and children alike. The dog's requirements are minimal and the perks of ownership maximum. Ideal for apartment dwellers and older folks who want a spunky alert companion who demands little more than love.

MINIATURE SCHNAUZER

German breeders developed the Miniature Schnauzer by mixing Affenpinscher and Poodle with the Standard Schnauzer, thus creating a small, sturdily built terrier exhibiting a rectangular head; strong, blunt muzzle, and small ears that may be cropped to stand erect or left natural to fold forward. Body is nearly square in outline. Tail customarily docked. Coat is hard and wiry, with fairly thick furnishings on the face, legs, and chest. Color can be solid black, salt and pepper, and black and silver. Height: 12–14 inches.

No longer the relentless vermin exterminator, the Miniature Schnauzer today is one of the world's most popular companion dogs. These smart-looking dogs are viably one-person dogs who require substantial attention, for fun and coat care. Socializing the puppy is akin to

A soft heart in a hard coat, the Miniature Schnauzer scraps its reputation as a rat killer and enjoys the embrace of pet life.

developing a well-mannered, all-accepting pet animal. As show-ring and obedience performers, the Mini is tops!

NEWFOUNDLAND

Developed on the shores of wintry Newfoundland, this large, heavily coated, very powerful breed has proven an indispensable work and rescue dog, not to mention companion, to man. Standing 26–28 inches tall and weighing 110–150 pounds, the Newfoundland possesses massive bone; broad, massive head; and deep chest. Ears are small and carried close to the head. Tail, of moderate length, is well covered with hair. Coat is of medium length, very dense, lying flat to the body. Color can be solid black, bronze, or particolor (known as Landseer).

A rather elegant bear of a dog, the Newfoundland ranks among the best outdoorsmen. Exercise and entertainment are musts as these dogs easily become idle and blue if unattended. They are excellent swimmers and are famed backpackers. Children and other pets get along grandly with the Newfy. Owners might be warned that this dog seems to think he's a lap dog and doesn't know his own strength—a true teddy bear with a polar bear appetite.

NORFOLK AND NORWICH TERRIERS

The Norfolk and the Norwich Terriers descend from general farm and hunting terriers commonly employed in Britain during the 1800s. Ears are the key distinguishing features of the breeds: the Norfolk is distinctive for his small, neatly dropped ears; the Norwich, for his erect ears of medium size, set well apart, with pointed tips. Show people will point out other distinctions. They are among the smallest of functional terriers, standing 10 inches tall and weighing 11–12 pounds. Coat is hard, and wiry, lying flat and close to the body and naturally weather-resistant. Color ranges from red to wheaten in the Norfolk; red, wheaten, black and tan, or grizzle in the Norwich.

Among the most familiar of terriers is the Norwich Terrier, a small British breed with smarts and determination to "out-pester any pest."

The Norfolk and Norwich Terriers are quality companion terriers. These easycare breeds require little in the way of coat care and exercise. They are spunky and loyal, good with older children and especially recommended for seniors. Alert and self-maintaining, the Norwich and Norfolk Terriers fit into smaller homes and make fine family dogs.

NORWEGIAN ELKHOUND

Proud and undaunted, the Norwegian Elkhound accompanied Vikings and traces to 4000–5000 B.C. He is a squarely built and well-

balanced dog, with a broad head; small, erect ears; and a tail curled tightly over his back. Chest is deep and moderately broad; legs, substantial but not coarse. His height is 17–20.5 inches; his weight, 44–55 pounds. Coat is thick, dense and hard; it lies close to the body and is longest on the back of the neck, buttocks, and underside of tail. Color is gray, with medium shades preferred.

The Old English Sheepdog or Bobtail unfurls a fun-loving, people-oriented temperament.

The Elkhound comes from a long line of dogs that were developed in close association with humans. Today's breed still thrives on the company of people and even prefers humans to canines. He is a good watchdog because he is stringently loyal. While time spent indoors with the family molds the dog's personality, this dog needs to be outdoors for fresh air and exercise.

OLD ENGLISH SHEEPDOG

Most distinctive for his long, profuse coat and bobbed tail (he sometimes is simply called the Bobtail), the OES first served man as a drover dog in the eighteenth century. He stands at least 22 inches tall and weighs 66 pounds or more. He possesses a roomy, square skull; medium-sized, flatly carried ears; rather short, very compact body, and round, muscular hindquarters. Puppies are either born tailless or docked at a few days of age. Coat is long, shaggy, and free from curl. Color can be any shade of gray, grizzle, blue, or blue merle, with or without white markings.

A superbly adaptable dog that does not require extensive care to maintain, the Old English Sheepdog is a bouncy affectionate companion. Climate and living conditions present little concern to the OES, and he makes due in most any space and clime. His natural biddability allows an owner to train him as a sled dog, herding dog, retriever, obedience and agility worker; plus he's a great show dog and pet. Yes, some grooming time is involved, and he sheds, sheds, sheds in due season.

OTTERHOUND

This old breed of hound was bred specifically to hunt otter in the waters of his native Great Britain. His sizable, symmetrical construction is well covered with a medium-length, hard, crisp coat, which is three–six inches long on the back, shorter on the rest of his body. Head is large and fairly narrow; muzzle, long and square, with powerful jaws and deep flews. Height: 23–27 inches. Weight: 65–120 pounds. Color typically grizzle or wheaten, though black and tan, liver and tan, and tricolor dogs also occur.

Mostly a hunting dog and water worker, the Otterhound is not recommended for the pet owner and particularly not for the new dog owner. These dogs need solid training administered by a credible authority. The Otterhound is perceptive and affectionate. He works and

plays hard, enjoys children, eats a ton, and needs a lot of land to run, and water to swim!

PAPILLON

Named for his unique butterfly-like ears (*papillon* is French for butterfly), which are large and erect, the Papillon represents the modernized dwarf spaniel of centuries-ago Europe. When the dog possesses

The Papillon is a tiny toy dog with a healthy outlook on life and a genuine appreciation for his keepers' attention.

drop ears, it may be called a Phalene (which means moth in French). He stands an elegant 8–11 inches tall. His construction is light and dainty. Head, small. Tail is long, carried well arched over the body. Coat is long, fine and silky, with plenty of fringe on chest, ears, tail and legs. Color is white with patches of any color except liver. A white blaze on the head is essential to the proper Papillon appearance.

Paps are not yappy, though they tend to be boisterous, playful and rather independent. This is a handsome, elegant toy dog that adapts well to a variety of living conditions. The Papillon does not resist pampering yet is never spoiled by it or expectant of it. Grooming concerns are noteworthy though not excessive. Children who know how not to step on a small dog make good friends.

PEKINGESE

The lion-like Pekingese undoubtedly stems from dogs once held sacred in China. His resemblance to the lion comes from his massive, broad skull; wide, black nose; body that is heavy in front, with deep chest, and lighter behind; and, importantly, his profuse, long, straight and harsh coat, with heavy feather-

An alert and fast-thinking muffin of a toy dog, the Pekingese needs supervision and considerable guidance.

ing (forming a ruff around the neck) and abundant undercoat. All colors occur; black masks and spectacles around the eyes are ideal. He is a short-legged dog and weighs under 14 pounds.

A self-assured, low-key house dog, the Peke offers much personality and attitude in an attractive Oriental package. The Peke's long coat demands attention on a daily basis. Boisterous, grabby children are not tolerated well by the Peke, nor are athletic or jogging adults. Supervision is recommended as Pekes can make trouble for themselves even in the tidiest homes.

PEMBROKE WELSH CORGI

This moderately long, low-set Welshman descends from old herding dogs who moved cattle by nipping their heels. He stands 10–12 inches tall and weighs a sturdy 24–28 pounds. Roughly resembling his Cardigan cousin, the Pembroke is distinctive for his "foxlike" look, created by his wedge-shaped head and firm, erect ears. Tail is docked as short as possible. Coat, medium length, short, dense, with a slighter thicker and longer ruff around the neck, chest and shoulders. Color can be red, sable, fawn, black and tan; solid or with white markings.

A quick-thinking, quick-to-learn dog, the Pembroke Welsh Corgi is a lot of dog in a small carton. He possesses a grand no-problem approach to life, able to herd bigger dogs and rowdy kids in a single

Fabulous PBGVs as puppies. This little French basset hound sports a wire coat and an electrical personality.

bound. Pembies tend to be a little nippy if surprised or mistreated. Convinced of their own importance, this Corgi has much personality to offer the right family.

PETIT BASSET GRIFFON VENDEEN

This compact, short-legged hound wearing a long, rough jacket descends from some of the oldest of hounds native to the Vendee regions of France. He is a strong, active dog, standing 13–15 inches and weighing 25–35 pounds. Head is of medium length, oval when viewed from front; ears fold inward, ending in an oval shape. Tail, medium in length, carried proudly "like

Pharaoh Hound

a saber," and well furnished. Coat color can be various shades of orange, gray, tawny, or black and tan, usually as spots on a white background.

A relative newcomer to the English-speaking purebred-dog world, the Petit Basset Griffon Vendeen (easier: PBGV) is an outgoing, tousled basset hound whose appeal as a pet and show dog seems truly endless. Presently the breed is being promoted in the U.S. and England (where they're called Roughies). Like certain other basset hounds, the dogs require a firm hand as they are too smart to easily slip into blind obedience.

PHARAOH HOUND

He is an ancient Egyptian dog of the wind whose ancestors can be found ceremoniously buried in the Nile Valley. Standing 21–25 inches tall, the breed depicts grace, balance, and great speed. Head is long, lean, and has a chiseled appearance; ears, erect, broad at the base, fine and large. Body is lithe, well-muscled, and cleanly outlined; legs, strong; tail, fairly long and tapering. The coat is short and glossy, ranging from fine and close to slightly harsh with no feathering. Color is tan with or without limited white markings.

A rare dog to see and rarer to catch, the Pharaoh Hound is a sleek and affectionate companion who is distinctly clean and easy to care for. Not the most flashy of the sight-

hound breeds, the Pharaoh Hound is more moderately sized than many of his running brethren and is notably more playful. Exercise is akin to survival.

POINTER

Pointers first appeared in England in 1650; their task was (and still is) to work with a hunter and "point out" the game. The Pointer undoubtedly looks sporty, with clean, medium-sized "dish-faced" head; deep muzzle; strong and solid back; and deep chest. Tail tapers and should not be so long as to reach hock, nor be docked. Height: 23–38 inches. Weight: 45–75 pounds. Coat is short, dense, and smooth, with a natural sheen. Color can be liver, lemon, black, orange, either solid or with white.

A mild-mannered hunting dog who lives to work and is rarely kept by persons who lack intentions of hitting the field. The breed's numbers are not as moderate as AKC/KCGB registrations would have them appear, as most dogs are used for hunting and field trialing and not showing. The dogs are clean and easily trainable to perform their namesake task.

POMERANIAN

Selectively bred from European herding-spitz-type dogs, the Pom gained favor in the 1700s under the motherly interest of Queen Victoria. Two centuries have brought us a considerably smaller Pom, standing no more than 11 inches and weighing 3–7 pounds. Head is wedge-shaped but not domed, having a fox-like expression. Back is short and level; body is cobby and rounded. The abundant double coat is short, soft and thick underneath; longer, coarse, and glistening outer. The Pom can be any solid color, or with lighter or darker shadings, or sable or black shadings; also in particolor, sable, and black/tan.

The Pomeranian knows that he is the epitome of the small dog and must yap a lot to prove it. These are full-coated, full-bodied spirits who are noted for curiosity and vivacity. The coat requires daily grooming to keep at its best. The breed's temperament is spitz through and through: self-assured, independent and alert.

POODLES

These forever-popular, world-renowned dogs originated in Europe. Of course, there are three varieties of Poodles: the Standard (the oldest) stands over 15 inches tall and weighs 45–70 pounds; the Miniature stands 10–15 inches; and the Toy stands under 10 inches. All three demonstrate remarkably similar conformation, sporting a profuse, dense, closely curling coat, which will cord if not combed. Color can be any solid color. Though parti-colored Poodles occur, they are not registerable, and most frowned upon by serious breeders.

One either loves or disdains Poodles. The three recognized sizes in the English-speaking world make somewhat different pets. The Standard is the most unique of the three, as he is a strong, sturdy dog with a confident air. The two smaller varieties seem more dependent on attention, yet no less confident. Although they do not shed, grooming needs are extensive with all varieties and the dogs are too intelligent to be ignored and enjoy people tremendously.

Poodles are popular show dogs. They require more preparation than any other dog in order to compete in the ring.

PORTUGUESE WATER DOG

This ages-old, faithful companion and co-worker of Portuguese fishermen descends from hardy water-dog stock, likely of like ancestry to the Poodle. He stands 16–22 inches and weighs a solid 35–55 pounds. Head is medium-sized, with ears carried down. Tail is carried loosely over the back. His distinctive shiny coat can be either wavy and loosely curled, or thick with shorter curls. Color can be solid white; black or liver, with or without white markings.

A gregarious, good-humored, and gifted water dog and pet, the Portie is an individualist. The breed is easily trained as a retriever, is loyal enough to function as a guard dog, and affectionate enough to be a most reliable companion. Exercise must be guaranteed or else the Portie gets portly.

PUG

The Pug's compact design reveals his true ancestry: he is a miniaturized mastiff who has existed for ages. The Pug stands 10–11 inches tall and weighs 14–18 pounds. The round head is large and massive in comparison to his short, cobby body. Muzzle is short, blunt, and square, but not upturned; ears, small, thin, and folded. Distinctive wrinkles adorn the head. Tail is curled as tightly as possible over the hip. Coat, short and smooth, fine and glossy. Color can be silver or apricot-fawn, with clearly defined markings.

Pugs require lots of attention and discipline as they are strong-willed and industrious. The breed is a hardy dog given the proper exercise and diet. Children should find a more suitable playmate since Pugs are

For such a small dog, the Pug is rock-solid with a tough mind to match. Discipline is in order lest your Pug be unruly and disorderly.

The Hungarian Puli is a mass of cords, energy and know-how.

not particularly disposed to youthful antics. Older folk living in any environment wisely welcome the Pug, provided that a little snoring and snorting doesn't keep them up at night.

PULI

The Hungarian Puli, like his larger Komondor countryman, wears a similar corded coat, which is long, thick, coarse, and heavy. Unlike the Komondor, however, the Puli can be groomed so as to prevent cording. The Puli is 14–19 inches tall and weighs 18–39 pounds. Overall, he is a compact, well-balanced dog of square appearance. Tail is carried over the back, blending with the level backline. The Puli can be rusty black, black, any shade of gray, and white, all in solid colors only.

In order to convey the true Puli appearance, a corded coat really is essential. Therefore, much time in maintaining the cords will be required. Pulik are noted for their high intelligence and high energy. Apartment life is too prison-like for the Puli and lots of room outdoors is needed. These are natural working dogs that enjoy finding new outlets for their energy and talents.

RHODESIAN RIDGEBACK

This breed originated in Africa during the 1500–1600s as a result of crosses of native African and "immigrant" European dogs. He is a hardy and courageous dog, standing 24–27 inches and weighing 65–75 pounds. Head of fair length, flat and broad between the medium-sized, tapering and hanging ears. Chest, very deep and capacious. His back bears his distinctive ridge, formed by hair growing in the opposite direction to the rest of the coat. Coat is short, dense, sleek and glossy. Color, light to red wheaten.

An agile and strong canine, the Rhodesian Ridgeback is an adult's dog that requires considerable training to survive as a house dog. Outdoor life agrees with the Rhodesian and some breed members do not tolerate children. As watchdogs, they are reliable and capable. Grooming and feeding are only moderately demanding.

ROTTWEILER

The Rottweiler, a descendent of ancient Roman mastiffs, has been around for many centuries, but it is only recently that the breed has gained its tremendous popularity. A large and powerful breed, the Rottie stands 22–27 inches tall and weighs 90–110 pounds. Skull is broad be-

tween the ears, preferably without wrinkles; cheekbones, well developed. Ears are proportionately small, triangular, hanging close to the head. Neck, powerful. Tail is customarily docked short to the body. Coat: straight, coarse, and dense. Color is invariably black with tan markings.

A well-bred Rottweiler is a soundly built, courageous animal, trustworthy and kind. This powerful dog must be properly trained in order to channel his seemingly endless talents in positive directions. The breed's popularity presents problems to buyers, and British owners must be aware of national laws about the keeping of this breed. The Rottie is affectionate with the whole family and will protect his own with his life. Outdoor life is a plus as this is an athlete par excellence.

A dog as powerful as an adult Rottweiler requires proper training and supervision. Ideally this breed is gentle and consistent with children.

SAINT BERNARD

Believably descended from heavy Asian mastiffs brought to Switzerland by the passing Roman legions, the Saint Bernard emerged as the premier search-and-rescue dog of Europe. Among the largest of all dog breeds, he stands 25.5–27.5 inches and weighs 110–200-plus pounds; his general appearance is powerful, strong and muscular. Two coat varieties occur: a long, of medium length, straight to slightly wavy hair; and a short, of very dense, smooth, tough hair. Color is invariably red and white (or white and red).

Ideally the Saint Bernard is a loving, well-mannered dog who listens attentively to his master's every command—and obeys. Discipline and socialization from an early age are required to acquire a Saint Bernard as described. These are very large dogs with big appetites and large outdoor requirements. Grooming is not terribly demanding, even for the longhaired variety.

SALUKI

The graceful and symmetrical Saluki traces to the ancient Middle East. He stands a lean 23–28 inches tall, with bitches possibly shorter. Head is long and narrow; ears long and covered with silky hair. Neck is long; chest, deep and moderately narrow. Coat is smooth and silky, with feathering on legs, back of thighs, tail and ears; or completely smooth and free from feathering.

Samoyed puppy showing off the standard breed smile!

Aloof with strong instincts, the Saluki is not the choice of just any dog owner. These dogs are not typically affectionate with people until they are familiar with them. They retain a high degree of independence and need much daily exercise to stay toned and mentally fit. Salukis remain prey-oriented and will likely snag the family rabbit or gerbil, so these small mammal types should certainly be avoided or kept from the Saluki.

SAMOYED

The Samoyed descends from rugged Northern herding dogs, hardy workers who served man as hunter, herder, and guardian. Yet, for all this working quality, the Sammy sports a beautiful long, white or biscuit, off-standish coat, with dense underwool. This coat, free from curl, forms a dense ruff around the neck and shoulders. Typically spitz-like, the head is wedge-shaped; the ears, erect triangles; tail, carried loosely curled over the back. Height: 19–23.5 inches. Weight: 50–65 pounds.

Smiling and friendly, the Samoyed has provided man with loving companionship for many centuries. The history of this dog has always been tied to his people who prized the dog first as a companion, and then as a worker. The Samoyed's coat is wonderfully easy to care for, despite its plushness and whiteness. These are strong dogs that require moderate exercise and food. Owners in warm climates ought reconsider keeping the Samoyed.

SCHIPPERKE

The Schipperke descends from mid-sized herding dogs of Belgium, from which he was developed to serve as a compact watchdog, weighing today no more than 18 pounds. His head is fox-like, fairly wide and narrowing at the eyes; ears are small, triangular, and carried erect. Body is short and cobby. Tail is docked to no more than one inch in length. The abundant coat is fairly short on the body, longer around the neck, forming a ruff; between the front legs, forming a jabot; and the rear, forming culottes or pants. Color in the U.S. is solid black only, with other solid colors accepted in Europe.

For the pet owner, the Schipperke is a super find. This is a competent watchdog, an active running mate, and an all-around athlete of a dog in a most conveniently sized package. Plus the Schip is playful, delightful and sweet-spirited. The breed needs plenty of attention and has more than a tad of energy to expend on a daily basis. Coat care is a breeze.

SCOTTISH DEERHOUND

Bred centuries ago in Scotland, the breed developed into the finest deer hunter in dogdom. He is a lean dog, rather tall, often described as a wire-coated Greyhound of heavier bone. Height is 28–32 inches; weight, 75–110 pounds. Head, appearing long, tapers to the eyes, and increasingly to the nose; muzzle, pointed. Neck, long, with a mane formed by the coat. Tail, rather long, tapering, well covered with hair. Coat on the body is harsh and wiry, between three and four inches long; it is much softer on the head, breast and belly. Color can be a variety of self colors and brindles, with dark blue-gray most highly valued.

"Gentleness, strength, dignity and courage" are the qualities frequently ascribed to the Deerhound. These graceful creatures need much room to stretch their long limbs, as one would imagine. Patience tops the list of training necessities and the

Deerhound's spirit can be injured by harsh scolding. The Deerhound is a kind soul that deserves reciprocal generous care.

SCOTTISH TERRIER

The Scottie emerged suddenly in the mid-1800s as a show dog, but it is believed that long before that time he served man as only a true terrier could. Though a small dog, standing only 10–11 inches and weighing 19–23 pounds, he is a canine of power, substance, and performance. Head is long and of medium width; ears, small, rather pointed, carried erect. Body is moderately short, indicating strength. The shortish coat is extremely hard and wiry. Color can be black, brindle, wheaten, gray, or grizzle.

Enjoying moderate popularity around the world, the Scottish Terrier has been described as the terrier man's terrier. His coat is distinctly wire and requires stripping, though pet owners often opt to clip the coat. As a sportsman, the Scottie is a force to be reckoned with: he has been effectively worked on rat, rabbit, and partridge; as a ferreter, retriever, and gundog. At home he is sensible, affectionate and alert.

Schipperkes are the right size for many folks! This little black Belgian offers colorful big-dog possibilities.

SEALYHAM TERRIER

Packing a lot of courage into a small package, Captain John Owen Tucker developed what he thought to be the ideal terrier, namely the Sealyham. A short though strong and substantial dog, the breed stands 10–11 inches and weighs 22–25 pounds. Head is long, broad, and powerful; with ears folded level with top of head. Neck should be slightly less than two-thirds the

ming and plucking. Overall the breed is friendly and makes a great watchdog.

SHAR-PEI

This most-wrinkled dog in the world traces to China, where he served as a hunter, herder, protector, and fighter. Height: 18–20 inches. Weight: 45–55 pounds. His distinctive muzzle is moderately long, broad from eyes to nose, with-

length of body, which is equal to the dog's height. His double coat is hard and wiry on top, soft and dense below. Color can be all white, or with lemon, tan or badger markings on head and ears.

Although most Sealyhams would opt for working the ground given their muddy druthers, the dogs today are primarily home pets and show dogs. They still maintain lots of terrier tenacity and take rather little teasing from toddlers. The coat requires grooming, including trim-

A colorful litter of Shar-Pei puppies, wrinkled and ready-to-go!

out any taper. Ears, very small, folded. Tongue, a bluish black color. Tail, carried high and curved, in a tight curl, or curled over. Characteristic are loose skin and a frowning expression. Two coat types: short, bristly and off-standish (horse coat); and slightly longer (brush coat). Color can be solids in black, red, shades of fawn, and cream.

The disarming and chic appeal of a Shar-Pei puppy must be blamed for the destruction of many breed members by ill-informed pet owners. Owners must be aware of the breed's potential skin and eye problems, which good breeders work hard to eliminate. Shar-Pei are quarrelsome with other dogs and tend to be one-person dogs. Also note that the dogs do not transfer well to second homes—consider this breed carefully.

SHETLAND SHEEPDOG

This diminutive collie descends from a variety of hardy working dogs, bantamized on the rugged Shetland Islands to work the similarly diminutive stock. Standing 13–16 inches tall, the Sheltie closely resembles the Collie in appearance. Head, refined in shape, appears as a long, blunt wedge, tapering slightly from ears to nose. Eyes, almond shaped; ears, small, carried three-quarters erect and tipping forward. Body appears moderately long, with deep chest and muscular back. Coat is long, dense, and harsh, with abundant undercoat; it forms a mane and frill around the neck. Color: black, blue merle, and sable, marked with white and/or tan.

The Sheltie is always tuned in to your channel. His family is his flock, and he feels a definite responsibility for the well-being of every member ... but he is a one-man dog. The other members of his human flock are treated according to their rela-

tionship with the master/shepherd. Strangers are announced and then greeted with reserved dignity. They will endure the attention of little people and kittens with admirable stoicism, but will generally try to stay out of their way. Nimble and energetic, the Sheltie is always ready to go out and play, but is just as happy to lay quietly at your feet at day's end.

Shelties are endearing and sensitive, providing nary a dull moment for attentive owners.

SHIBA INU

A sharp-minded, most attractive miniature spitz breed from Japan, the Shiba Inu sports small prick ears, a curled tail, off-standish coat and a Nordic face. The breed should look like a small-version Japanese Akita. The Shiba can be red, red-sesame or black and tan. He stands 13–16 inches and weighs 20–30 pounds.

A "cat" in wolf's clothing, the Shiba is highly independent, clean, and smarter than most dog trainers. This is the perfect choice for apartment and city dwellers and likely the prettiest face on any block. Very primitive and often stubborn, the Shiba is quiet, reserving its characteristic squeal-like voice. Still somewhat rare, so quality specimens will demand a good price.

stands 9–10.5 inches tall, typically weighing 12–15 pounds. Head is broad and round, wide between the large, round eyes; ears, large, long, carried drooping. Body is longer than high, with broad, deep chest. He is adorned with long, dense coat, which may be slightly wavy. The Shih Tzu can be all colors.

Once more the choice of the lady of the house, the Shih Tzu today has countless fans of both genders. The dog's warm, endearing personality

SHIH TZU

Shih Tzu translates from the Chinese as "lion," and these tiny lion-like dogs were prized members of the Chinese court, some thousand years back. The proud Shih Tzu

The Shih Tzu is a lovable, people-loving dog with a bouncy and flexible approach to daily life.

Siberian Husky puppies getting a feel for the slope of the sled. Many Huskies today are still used for sled-pulling, and sled-dog competitions are growing very common.

and his genuine good looks make him the perfect home companion. The coat, if intended for showing, will require a great deal of time; a pet clip is easier to maintain and leaves the dog looking furry and soft. Shih Tzus generally don't mind a toddler's toting them about and enjoy the attention most of the time. Some breed members are truly teddy bears, others maintain the mystery of the koalas.

SIBERIAN HUSKY

The Siberian Husky is an ancient breed whose direct ancestors were enduring sled dogs of the Chukchi people of northeastern Asia. A medium-sized, moderately compact dog, the Husky stands 21–23.5 inches tall and weighs 45–60 pounds. Head is slightly rounded on top, tapering to the eye; ears medium-sized erect triangles. Chest, deep; back, straight and strong. Tail, a well-furred fox-brush. Coat is medium-length and double; plentiful but not obscuring. All colors from black to pure white (including grays, reds, and pieds occur) on the Husky pattern; facial mask is characteristic.

This extroverted, inexhaustible dog requires no small amount of exercise time. Siberians can run for hours, and enjoy frolicking with their owners. He is generally independent but also gregarious with his fellow dogs. Despite his dense coat, he is very clean and devoid of doggy odor. A life indoors is tantamount to misery — this dog needs to be outdoors and does well in a kennel environment.

SILKY TERRIER

The Silky was developed in the early 1900s from selective Australian crossbreeding of the Australian and Yorkshire Terriers. He is a hardy dog, though definitely of small size, standing 9 inches and weighing 8–10 pounds. Head is wedge-shaped and moderately short; ears, small, V-shaped, and carried erect. Body is low-set, slightly longer than high. Tail, docked, is set high and carried erect or semi-erect. Coat is 5–6 inches long, lying flat; fine, glossy and silky in appearance and texture; unlike the Yorkie's, it should not touch the floor.

A tiny terrier whose coat is silky does not know the joys of ratting, despite certain reports of success. The Silky Terrier was brought into existence to be a pet, and does his designated job very well. Spirited and friendly by definition, the breed is a mannerly, loving companion for the elderly and children alike. The coat requires brushing but is not a nuisance to upkeep.

SKYE TERRIER

Of colorful and debatable history, this distinctive terrier traces to Great Britain, where it has been enjoyed for many centuries. Standing only 9.5–10 inches and weighing 25 pounds, the Skye combines a certain elegance with solid bone and hard muscle. Head is long and powerful; ears, distinctively feathered, carried either erect or drop. Neck, long and arched. Legs, short. Body, long and low. His coat is hard, long (about 5.5 inches), and straight. Color can be solid black, various grays, fawn, or cream.

The Skye is a proper canine, even-tempered and predictable. With strangers, the breed prefers to be stand-offish and does not relish excessive handling. Owners find much to recommend in the Skye: they are long-lived, hardy, very loyal and require little in the way of exercise and food. The coat requires regular grooming to keep looking its best.

A terrier with a remarkable coat, the Skye Terrier promises blue skies to its owner on even the grayest of gray days.

SOFT COATED WHEATEN TERRIER

A hardy, well-balanced sporting terrier, the Soft Coated traces to Ireland, where he was a dog of the poor, maintained for his utility. He stands 18–19 inches tall and weighs a compact 35–45 pounds. His distinctive, unterrier-like coat is soft and silky, not harsh, and profuse. Head is rectangular in appearance. Ears, small to medium, break level with the skull. Color can be any shade of wheaten, from light wheaten to golden reddish wheaten (commonly darker in puppies, lighter in adolescents). Proper coat takes up to two years to develop.

This tall-standing, well-adjusted pet terrier and show-ring star is far more sweet-natured than many of the other terriers—a real pert for a dog this size. Wheatens love to run and let their soft hair blow in the wind. The soft coat of the Wheaten does not shed but requires consistent grooming. Overall this is a non-aggressive dog that loves attention and activity.

STAFFORDSHIRE BULL TERRIER

Tracing to the rugged bulldogs and game terriers of England, this bull-and-terrier breed emerged in the 1800s as a fighting dog. Considerably mellowed over the years, the Staff stands 14–16 inches tall and weighs 24–38 pounds. Head is short, deep; with broad skull and pronounced cheek bones. Ears, rose-

The Soft Coated Wheaten Terrier is a full-bearded bloke with a full flask of goodwill and gaiety.

shaped or half-pricked; not large. Body, large in front, lighter behind. Coat is short, smooth, and close to the skin. Color can be red, fawn, white, black, blue, or brindle; with or without white markings.

Sensible and affectionate, the Staffordshire Bull Terrier requires an intelligent and strict owner who understands the nature of these dogs. Staffs are aggressive with other dogs, though never with people. The breed does not stir commotion on its own, but sure can defend himself. The breed enjoys a large British following and is smaller than the American Staffordshire Terrier, a dog not well known in England, though quite common in the States.

STANDARD SCHNAUZER

The Standard Schnauzer believably traces to fifteenth-century Germany, where smooth-coated German Pinschers were crossed with heavier-coated dogs to obtain this robust working dog. He served as the prototype for his two "brother" breeds, the Miniature and Giant Schnauzers. Head is strong and rectangular. Ears, medium in size, cropped and carried erect, or natural and folded. Body, square, substantial, and compact. Tail, carried erect, is docked to be one to two inches. His rough wiry coat is tight, hard, and as thick as possible. Color can be salt and pepper, or solid black. Not a popular companion in the English-speaking world, this German workman is a jack of all trades and an affectionate pet animal. The breed is able to exterminate, guard, and herd, among other doggy chores. Many Standards make good show dogs and they are adaptable and obedient. Grooming and clipping are required for the show dog.

SUSSEX SPANIEL

The massive and muscular Sussex Spaniel traces to a single British kennel, which fostered the breed during the 1800s. Low-set and very substantial, the Sussex stands 13–15.5 inches tall and weighs 40–45 pounds. Head is moderately long and wide, with fairly heavy brows. Ears are thick, fairly large, carried close to the head. Chest is round, deep, and wide. Back is long and very muscular. Tail is docked to 5–7 inches. The flat-lying silky-textured coat is moderately long, with abundant feathering. Color is solid golden liver, without any white.

An adorable huntsman, the Sussex is a low-standing, low-on-the-totem-pole spaniel known for his determination, if not his speed. Rarely a problem to train and good-humored, easygoing companions, Sussexes are not too numbersome but sustain an even following for they are truly a unique and worthwhile breed. Exercise is encouraged, as is a sensible diet.

TIBETAN SPANIEL

Of mysterious and unknown beginnings, the Tibetan Spaniel traces to the Orient. Though standing only 10 inches tall and weighing 9–15 pounds, he is no toy dog either. Head is small in proportion to body, which is slightly longer than tall. Ears are medium sized, set high, and pendant; well feathered with fur. Neck hair forms a mane or "shawl." Tail, well plumed, is carried in a curl over the back. Coat is double, moderately long on body, lying flat, silky in texture. All colors occur.

An agile and assertive little dog, the Tibetan Spaniel, of course, is not spaniel, but rather a smart and trusting companion animal. This very authentic purebred lacks the physical exaggeration that attracts and disdains many to and from the Pekingese and Pug. The breed's temperament makes it a fine choice for anyone seeking a loyal, sweet and family-oriented dog.

TIBETAN TERRIER

Despite his name, the Tibetan Terrier is not a terrier but a true and very old herding dog, developed in his native Tibet from ancient indigenous working-dog types. He is a rugged dog who stands 14–16 inches tall and weighs a lean 18–30 pounds. Ears are V-shaped and pendant, very well feathered. Body is compact and powerful, with a medium-length, well-feathered tail carried over the back. His distinctively long, shaggy coat covers his face; this coat can be either straight or waved. All colors are perfectly acceptable.

The Tibetan Terrier has much to recommend him to the Western dog lover. This mid-sized Oriental cavorter is a highly adaptable, healthy and affectionate companion animal designed (and maybe guaranteed) to bring luck and love to any family.

Adorable and furry, the Tibetan Terrier fits into any home with an open door.

The breed is playful and energetic, like any bouncy Tibetan, and requires exercise time. Grooming should not be overlooked.

TOY FOX TERRIER

This breed directly descends from the Smooth Fox Terrier. He was developed through selective breeding in the 1800s. Known also as the AmerToy, he is a well-constructed tot of a terrier, standing 10 inches

Vizsla

and weighing a mere 3.5–7 pounds. The breed is solidly constructed. Head tapers from ears to nose; ears, fairly large, carried erect. Chest deep. Tail, customarily docked short. Coat is short and smooth, preferably occurring in tricolor, with white predominating.

This American original is a broad-minded, all-accepting, easy-to-love toy breed which has remained a popular American choice for generations. In addition to being easy-to-love, they are also easy-to-groom, care-for, and maintain. These are inventive, showy dogs for most anyone, no matter of age, mobility or lifestyle.

VIZSLA

This is Hungary's pointer; his ancestors faithfully accompanied the Magyar settlers of that European region on hunts more than 1,000 years ago. Distinguished by his robust yet light build, the breed stands 22–24 inches tall and weighs 49–62 pounds. Head is lean and muscular. Neck, smooth and strong. Body, lean and muscular; back,

The Vizsla is a well-balanced working gun dog. Family life is high on this dog's list of priorities. He is even-tempered and enjoyable to be around.

The Welsh Terrier shines as a confident and eager companion dog. A medium-sized terrier, the Welshie is among the most beguiling and predictable of all breeds.

short. Coat is short, smooth, dense, and close-lying. A wirehaired variety occurs but is not registerable in the U.S. Color can be various shades of solid golden rust. Eye color, never yellow, should blend with coat.

Although the Vizsla is a reliable and much-revered hunter, the breed has won over many hearts as a family pet. As his name implies in Hungarian, the Vizsla is a *responsive* animal whose heart, like his coat, is pure gold. The breed is very active and needs regular exercise for muscle tone and a well-tuned temperament.

WEIMARANER

Blended in Germany from various gundog types, the Weimaraner has been hunting game at least since the 1600s. The breed today is a graceful, well-balanced dog whose conformation indicates his ability in the field. He stands 23–28 inches and weighs 70–85 pounds. Head is moderately long, labeled "aristocratic." Ears, long, slightly folded, set high. Body, moderate in length, and strong, with deep chest. Tail docked to about 6 inches. Coat is short, smooth and sleek, occurring in shades of mouse-gray to silver-gray only.

The allure of the "Gray Ghost" is mystic in itself. These are multi-talented working dogs with a keen desire to feel a part of the family routine. Not recommended for city life or apartment dwellings, the active Weimaraner needs space and time. The dogs excel in the show ring and obedience trials—no coincidence as they are intelligent, trainable and elusively beautiful.

WELSH SPRINGER SPANIEL

Long the principal gundog of Wales, the versatile Welsh Springer has been working over land and water for centuries. He is a very well-balanced and proportionate dog, weighing 35–45 pounds. Eyes hazel or dark in color; ears, set low and hanging close to the head. Body, not long, is strong and muscular. Tail, set low and lightly feathered, is never carried above the backline. Coat is either straight or flat and thick, with texture silky. Color invariably a dark rich red and white.

Teach this little guy young, say breeders of the Welsh Springer, who

is sometimes called the Starter. This tidy-sized gundog can be taught to work as well as the best of them. In numbers he is smaller than the Cocker and English Springer, though in ability and trainability, he is easily their equal. For apartment dwellers with a commitment to the dog's good health and exercise, the Welsh Springer leaps out as a sensible selection.

WELSH TERRIER

A descendant of the various proven terriers of the British Isles, the Welsh was developed in his native Wales as a sporting terrier of otter, fox, and badger hunting. Rugged, compact, and sturdy, he ideally stands 15 inches tall and weighs 20 pounds. Head is rectangular; ears, small, V-shaped, and folded forward. Tail docked to "complete the image of a square dog." Coat is hard, wiry and dense, forming a close-fitting, protective jacket. Color is black with tan markings on head, quarters, and legs; or grizzle.

For such a little dog, the Welshie has big ideas, which can be mistaken either for stubbornness or profundity. The dog is a spool of energy and needs to have good fun, especially since the business of chasing rats and badgers has scurried away from the modern breed. He is a fine house dog, once properly trained, and his personality endears him to terrier and non-terrier folk alike.

Although the Westie makes a top-notch show animal, the breed is kept by many families as "just pets." Westies continue to gain popularity for good reasons.

WEST HIGHLAND WHITE TERRIER

The Westie believably originated in Scotland; he is a hardy, strongly constructed dog of close relation to the Cairn, Scottish, and Dandie Dinmont Terriers. Compact and substantial, he measures 10–11 inches and registers 15–22 pounds. His distinctive and highly considered rough, wiry white coat consists of an inner and outer coat, which is straight and hard, about two inches long (shorter on neck and shoulders). Skull, fairly broad; ears, small, carried tightly erect. Tail, relatively short; when carried erect, it should not be higher than top of skull.

A choice family dog, the Westie is a well-rounded, well-suited canine that ranks high on our list of purebreds. The breed temperament is consistently adaptable, faithful and fun-loving. Children love Westies, and you would be hard-pressed to find a Westie who was not fond of any low-to-the-ground humans. The show coat requires grooming and professional sculpting, though excessive trimming is not required for the pet animal.

WHIPPET

The Whippet emerged in England during the late nineteenth century as a rabbit-coursing dog, created by crossing small Greyhounds with various terriers. Today's smaller and refined type owes much to later crosses to the Italian Greyhound. Standing 18–22 inches and weighing about 28 pounds, he is considered pound-for-pound the fastest dog on earth, often employed as a professional race dog. Head is long and lean; ears small, thrown back, and folded. Neck, long and clean. Topline of the back forms a graceful and natural arch. Tail, long and tapering. Coat is short, close, smooth and firm in texture. Color is not important.

A moderate-sized greyhound type, the Whippet is renowned for his speed: quick to run, quick to learn and quick to love (for a sighthound of course). Even in light of the small size, the breed should not be kept in an apartment setting, as it is far too active and tends to be a little jumpy. Active, well-balanced individuals make the most suitable companions for Whippets.

WIREHAIRED POINTING GRIFFON

Founder of the breed Edward Korthals crossed various pointers, setters, water dogs, and other gundogs during the late 1800s to produce this wirehaired hunter, also called the Korthals Griffon. Strong and vigorous, he stands 22–24 inches and weighs 50–60 pounds. Head, long, harshly coated. Body, strong; fairly short-backed. His tail is customarily docked to one-third and furnished with hard coat. Coat overall is hard, dry, and stiff (never curly), forming heavy beard and eye brows. Color: solid chestnut or chestnut with white or steel gray (roan) markings.

This exacting, hard-working hunter represents the high-quality Continental pointers with which American and British sportsmen have recently become acquainted. The Wirehaired Pointing Griffon not only makes a top-of-the-line hunter on a variety of terrains but also makes an active, affectionate pet. Exercise mandatory.

YORKSHIRE TERRIER

Once the English commoner's dog, the Yorkie gained "noble" popularity in the Victorian era and has ever since enjoyed universal appeal with all, regardless of social class. Once divided into two weight varieties, the breed today comes only in one, namely under 7 pounds; he stands about 9 inches tall. Head is small; ears, small, V-shaped, carried erect. Body, well proportioned, with back rather short. Tail is docked to a medium length and carried slightly higher than the level of the back. His distinctive toy-terrier coat is long and straight; glossy, fine, and silky. Color invariably blue and tan (puppies born black and tan).

Yorkies legitimately capture the essence of the toy breeds in one floor-reaching swoop! These are tiny, tiny dogs that require close supervision and very loving, devoted owners. As small dogs go, the Yorkie requires a great deal of attention to keep: the long coat, kept in the traditional floor-length show style, must be groomed daily and guarded against damage. Yorkies are a pocketful of spunk and are extremely loving and loyal best friends.

Sharing one's snacktime, naptime and lifetime with a Yorkie pal is sure to promise rewarding happiness for the right owner.

INDEX